MANAGING RISK
AND CREATING
VALUE WITH
MICROFINANCE

Managing Risk and Creating Value with Microfinance is available as an interactive textbook at **http://www.worldbank.org/pdt**. The electronic version allows communities of practice, colleagues working in sectors and regions, and students and teachers to share notes and related materials for an enhanced, multimedia learning and knowledge-exchange experience.

MANAGING RISK AND CREATING VALUE WITH MICROFINANCE

MIKE GOLDBERG AND ERIC PALLADINI

THE WORLD BANK
WASHINGTON, D.C.

ISBN: 978-0-8213-8228-8
eISBN: 978-0-8213-8235-6
DOI: 10.1596/978-0-8213-8228-8

Library of Congress Cataloging-in-Publication Data

Goldberg, Mike, 1956-
    Managing risk and creating value with microfinance / by Mike Goldberg and Eric Palladini.
        p. cm.
    Includes index.
    ISBN 978-0-8213-8228-8 -- ISBN 978-0-8213-8235-6 (electronic)
    1. Microfinance. 2. Risk management. I. Palladini, Eric, 1956- II. Title.
    HG178.3.G65 2010
    332--dc22

                                                                        2009052150

Cover photos: © Curt Carnemark and Julio Pantoja/The World Bank; Larry Mayorga/Pictionary Studio (top left and center)
Book/book cover design: Larry Mayorga/Pictionary Studio

Contents

FIGURES

MAP

TABLES

Preface
Results of a South American Dialogue Series

When World Bank staff members meet with representatives of a country's microfinance sector, microfinance institution (MFI) managers often assume that they will receive some kind of new financing—credit lines, guarantees, or grants—to support their development efforts. They do not expect the Bank to provide technical assistance or best-practice information.

More recently, however, representatives in four countries have observed that, in keeping with the World Bank's new role as a "knowledge bank," the Bank's new knowledge-sharing priorities mean that it can provide more than just new funding. It can provide access to recent developments in international best practices in microfinance management, build South-South learning dialogues, and address strategic and operational challenges. As a result of this realignment of Bank priorities, MFI managers have access to world-class expertise, innovative technologies, and tools in risk management.

This report brings together the results of an eight-part series of presentations by leading experts in issues directly related to microfinance institutional sustainability. It is intended for MFI board members, managers, and staff members—as well as for government regulators, supervisors, and donor staff members. The first four chapters include topics in risk management: (1) risk management systems, (2) good governance, (3) interest rates, and (4) microinsurance. The last four chapters include four topics in new product development and efficient delivery methodologies: (5) housing microfinance, (6) microleasing, (7) disaster preparedness products and systems, and (8) new technologies.

Microfinance practitioners and government supervisors and regulators in Bolivia, Colombia, Ecuador, and Peru participated in the presentations and discussions. In addition, a group of Argentine practitioners was able to view the presentations through simultaneous Webcasts. The objectives of the series were as follows:

- To strengthen MFIs by disseminating innovative approaches in risk management, cost control, governance, and new technologies
- To promote a South-South exchange of experiences and lessons learned
- To promote greater ties among the MFIs in the region and between MFIs and government supervisors and regulators
- To highlight the Bank's ability to mobilize international technical expertise in microfinance

The World Bank's move to engage with MFIs in the four countries began in 2006, which was a critical year for microfinance in Latin America. In that year, the Bank identified a new trend of financial sector policies—represented by newly elected governments in Bolivia and Ecuador—that would ultimately and artificially lower microfinance interest rates, interfere with the sustainability of MFIs, and reduce outreach. Rather than expanding product menus and introducing cost-saving technologies, the new governments sought to improve access to credit by mandating interest rates below the rate of inflation. Experience has shown that such a policy leads to credit diversion and a decrease in sustainable lending to microbusinesses and poor households.

In contrast, the Peruvian and Colombian governments moved to ensure the growth of a commercial microfinance industry through a number of sound regulatory and supervisory options. Given such developments, the Bank saw an opportunity to sponsor a broad policy dialogue with the policy makers and representatives of national microfinance industries to review policy options and new approaches. This book reflects the technical support and dialogue that developed.

Acknowledgments

The authors would like to thank a number of individuals and institutions that played a key role in carrying out this ambitious undertaking.

The Technology Backbone. Daniel de la Morena, David Gray, Claudia María Hernández, and Pablo Salinas of the World Bank's Global Development Learning Network (within the Development Effectiveness Unit of the Latin America and the Caribbean Region) were instrumental in providing technical support for the discussion sessions. Because there were usually nine distance learning centers in four countries and speakers in various countries, the logistical challenges were daunting. This team responded to every challenge efficiently and professionally.

The Global Development Learning Network (GDLN). The GDLN centers in the four countries also played a key role in facilitating the sessions. Those centers were GDLN Bolivia (La Paz and Santa Cruz); GDLN Colombia (Bogotá); GDLN Ecuador (Cuenca, Loja, and Quito); and GDLN Peru (Arequipa, Chiclayo, and Lima).

Financial Support. No such effort can succeed without financial support. Shirley Matzen and Roberto Tarallo of the Latin America and the Caribbean Region trust funds management team of the World Bank were instrumental in obtaining grant funds from the U.K. Department for International Development (DFID), through the Latin American Markets and International Trade (LAMIT) program grant facility. LAMIT generously provided the grant funds to cover the costs of organization and presentation of the series and for dissemination. The Bank team would especially like to recognize Graham Symons of DFID for his support.

National Microfinance Associations. The national microfinance associations were the clients for the presentations and technical discussions. Without their dedication and commitment to microfinance, the funds, technicians, and organization of the sessions would have been wasted. The World Bank team gratefully acknowledges the superb performance of the following institutions and leaders: Reynaldo Marconi, Asociación de Instituciones Financieras para el Desarrollo Rural (FINRURAL), Bolivia; Claudio Higueras, Cooperativa Emprender, Colombia; Juan Pablo Guerra, Unión de Cooperativas de Ahorro y Crédito del Sur (UCACSUR), Ecuador; Javier Vaca, Red Financiera Rural (RFR), Ecuador; and Ana Jiménez and Luís Ríos Henckell, Consorcio de Organizaciones Privadas de Promoción al Desarrollo de la Micro y Pequeña Empresa (COPEME), Peru.

The World Bank Team. Although this book is based on the experts' presentations, members of the World Bank team contributed significant additional technical material. Economist and microfinance expert Eugenio Peral organized the conferences and provided material on all the chapters. Microfinance consultant Tillman Bruett of Alternative Credit Technologies LLC wrote the chapter on governance. World Bank microinsurance consultant Ramanathan Coimbatore provided additional material on insurance. Microfinance consultants Lisa Taber and Reuben Summerlin contributed with their painstakingly thorough and very useful technical review.

The authors would also like to express their great appreciation to Erika Vargas (GDLN) and Larry Mayorga (Pictionary Studio) for their special attention and hard work and for their treatment of this book as if it were the only one. Denise Bergeron, Dina Towbin, and Stuart Tucker of the World Bank Office of the Publisher, helped eliminate the inevitable errors that arise during the writing and production process. The authors are very grateful for their attention to detail.

About the Authors and Contributors

Authors

Mike Goldberg is a senior private sector development specialist in the Private Sector Development and Finance Unit of the Latin America and Caribbean Region of the World Bank, with expertise in microfinance, small and medium-size enterprise development, competitiveness, and local economic development. He has worked on projects in East Africa, East Asia, Eastern Europe, Latin America, and South Asia, and he provides training to Bank staff members. Before coming to the World Bank, Mr. Goldberg worked with the Consultative Group to Assist the Poor.

Eric Palladini is a consultant and technical writer at the World Bank, where he has worked on a number of projects dealing with private sector development, privatization, and microfinance in Mexico, Nicaragua, and Trinidad and Tobago. He also worked with the International Finance Corporation on the inaugural Municipal Scorecard study in Lima, Peru.

Contributors

Given the high technical standards required for World Bank–sponsored training activities, the Bank team turned to leading international experts on each of the topics. The following experts contributed presentations and provided further opportunities for consultation as this book project evolved into its final form.

Carlos Arce is a lawyer and economist at the World Bank. He has more than 20 years of experience in agricultural policy and rural development and has worked on microfinance and competitiveness projects in Central America. Mr. Arce contributed to the microinsurance session.

Tillman Bruett is a co-founder of Alternative Credit Technologies LLC. He has 15 years of finance experience, including commercial banking and microfinance. He is currently working as a regional specialist for the United Nations Capital Development Fund in the South Pacific. Mr. Bruett contributed to the governance session, and was the author of the chapter on governance.

Juan Buchenau was a consultant with the Consultative Group to Assist the Poor and has since joined the World Bank as a senior financial sector specialist in the Finance and Private Sector Unit of the Latin America and the Caribbean Region. He has worked extensively on rural microfinance for a variety of governments and donor institutions in Africa, Eastern Europe, and Latin America and in the United States. Mr. Buchenau contributed to the interest rates session.

Hans Dellien is the director of Microfinance Products and Services at Women's World Banking. He has delivered technical services to microfinance institutions in Africa, Asia, Latin America, and the Middle East. Mr. Dellien contributed to the risk management session.

Juan Manuel Díaz Parrondo has been a member of the Board of Directors of the Instituto Dominicano de Desarrollo Integral since 2003 and the representative of the Foundation for Development Cooperation and Promotion of Relief Activities in the Dominican Republic. He is a microfinance specialist who focuses on portfolio management, microfinance institution ratings, impact evaluation, savings programs, and financial planning. Mr. Díaz contributed to the governance session.

Todd Farrington is a financial economist with 15 years of experience in microfinance and development. He was a founding partner of MicroRate, the first specialized rating agency for microfinance. He is currently vice president of ACCIÓN International, overseeing the development of debt capital markets between ACCIÓN and other financial actors in the microfinance sector. Mr. Farrington contributed to the governance session.

Fernando Fernández is director of the Access to Rural Finance for Microenterprises (AFIRMA) project in Mexico, which is administered by Development Alternatives Inc. (DAI) for the U.S. Agency for International Development. Before joining AFIRMA, he was deputy director for the Strengthening Access to Microfinance and Liberalization Task Order (SALTO) project while working with the Superintendency of Banks and Insurance in Ecuador. Mr. Fernández contributed to the risk management session.

Jesús Ferreyra is the managing director of Mibanco in Peru, one of the leading microfinance institutions in the Andean region. Mibanco has been particularly successful in housing microfinance and has developed a range of innovative products and delivery methods. Mr. Ferreyra contributed to the housing microfinance session.

Adrián González is a lead researcher with the Microfinance Information Exchange (MIX). Since 2004, he has been in charge of quantitative analysis of the databases collected by MIX. Mr. González contributed to the interest rates session.

Eduardo Gutiérrez is director of the nongovernmental organization titled National Ecumenical Development Association (ANED), and has led the organization's efforts to transform ANED into a leader in rural lending in Bolivia. Before joining ANED, he worked for 23 years at the Central Bank of Bolivia. Mr. Gutiérrez contributed to the microleasing session.

Alice Liu is an information and communications technology development specialist at Development Alternatives Inc. (DAI). Before joining DAI, she worked in the private sector as a senior product manager on wireless product launches for AT&T and Hawaiian Telcom. Ms. Liu contributed to the technology session.

Michael McCord is president of the Microinsurance Centre. He has extensive experience in banking, microfinance, and microinsurance. His specializations include institutional development for microinsurance, new product development, and assessment and analysis of microinsurance programs. Mr. McCord contributed to the microinsurance session.

Rochus Mommartz is an economist at the Boulder Institute of Microfinance with 15 years of experience in microfinance. He specializes in microfinance institution management and financial sector regulation. He is also a consultant to the investment committee of the ResponsAbility Global Microfinance Fund in Switzerland. Mr. Mommartz contributed to the risk management session.

Enrique Pantoja is a regional planner and sociologist at the World Bank where he works in the Agriculture and Rural Development Department, Latin America and the Caribbean Region. He has worked on a variety of development projects over the past 15 years across Latin America and South Asia. Mr. Pantoja contributed to the disasters and microfinance session.

Héctor Fernando Rivas Martínez served for more than 25 years as an expert for Banorte in Mexico, covering a variety of responsibilities such as mergers, process re-engineering, and development of new products. In 2005, he became the assistant general manager of the Financiera Solidaria (FINSOL) finance company and was in charge of business and product development. Mr. Rivas contributed to the microinsurance session.

Santiago Saavedra is executive vice president of the Red Transaccional Cooperativa in Ecuador and is a finance specialist for the World Council of Credit Unions. His work includes technical assistance in risk management for Women's World Banking, Swisscontact, and several cooperatives. Mr. Saavedra contributed to the risk management session.

Richard Shumann is a housing credit specialist with the Cooperative Housing Foundation in Silver Spring, Maryland. Before assuming that position, he was the director of marketing and new product development for ACCIÓN International. Mr. Shumann contributed to the housing microfinance session.

Hannah Siedek is managing director at ProCredit Bank Congo. At the time of the presentation, she was with Consultative Group to Assist the Poor's Technology Program, where she supported technology-enabled delivery channels for financial services. Ms. Siedek contributed to the technology session.

Narda Lizette Sotomayor Valenzuela is the department chief for microfinance institutional analysis at the Superintendency of Banks, Insurance, and Pension Funds of Peru. She is also a professor in the Department of Economics of the Pontificia Universidad Católica del Perú. Ms. Sotomayor contributed to the interest rates session.

Glenn Westley was a senior adviser for microenterprise with Inter-American Development Bank (IDB). After nearly 31 years at IDB, he became a senior adviser with the Consultative Group to Assist the Poor. Mr. Westley contributed to the microleasing session.

Abbreviations

ACODEP	Association of Micro, Small, and Medium Development Consultants (Asociación de Consultores para el Desarrollo de la Pequeña, Mediana, y Microempresa) (Nicaragua)
AFIRMA	Access to Rural Finance for Microenterprises (Mexico)
ANED	National Ecumenical Development Association (Asociación Ecuménica de Desarrollo) (Bolivia)
ATM	automated teller machine
BRAC	Bangladesh Rural Advancement Committee
BTM	biometric ATM
CAMEL	Capital Adequacy, Asset Quality, Management, Earnings, and Liquidity Management
CAT DDO	catastrophe risk DDO
CECAM	Savings and Agricultural Credit Cooperative Society (Caisses d'Epargne et de Crédit Agricole Mutuels) (Madagascar)
CEO	chief executive officer
CGAP	Consultative Group to Assist the Poor
CHF	Cooperative Housing Foundation
CMAC	Cajas Municipales de Ahorro y Crédito (Peru)
DAI	Development Alternatives Inc.
DDO	deferred drawdown option
FFP	Prodem Fondo Financiero Privado (Bolivia)
Finarca	Financiera Arrendadora Centroamericana, S.A. (Nicaragua)
FUNHAVI	Housing and Habitat Foundation (Fundación Habitat y Vivienda, A.C.) (Mexico)
IADB	Inter-American Development Bank
IDDI	Dominican Integrated Development Institute (Instituto Dominicano de Desarrollo Integral) (Dominican Republic)
IFC	International Finance Corporation
MFI	microfinance institution
MIS	management information system
MIV	microfinance investment vehicle
MIX	Microfinance Information Exchange
NGO	nongovernmental organization
OECD	Organisation for Economic Co-operation and Development
PDA	personal digital assistant
POS	point of sale
SIM	subscriber identity module
SOFOL	Limited Objective Financial Society (Sociedad Financiera de Objeto Limitado) (Mexico)
SPM	social performance management
VAT	value added tax

1 RISK MANAGEMENT: PREPARING FOR THE UNEXPECTED

*Living at risk is jumping off the cliff and
building your wings on the way down.*

*Ray Bradbury**

* Ray Bradbury, undated, http://www.brainyquote.com/quotes/authors/r/ray_bradbury.html.

In business, the only constant is change. In a world of change, successful businesses and financial institutions have learned that it is wise to be prepared for unexpected events, in other words, to manage risk. While risk management has been a part of business planning for large businesses and financial institutions for some time, it is a fairly new discipline among microfinance institutions (MFIs). This new focus is the result of recent crises and experiences and represents a new understanding of the importance of anticipating unexpected events, rather than merely reacting to them. This chapter reviews risk categories and measurement for financial institutions, additional risks confronting MFIs, ways to develop a risk management system, and special risks faced by rural MFIs.[1]

In the wake of recent tragedies, MFIs around the world have had to cope with an array of financial, political, and weather-related crises, and MFI managers have learned the importance of risk management. For example, hurricanes in Nicaragua, floods in Poland, and currency crises in the Russian Federation and Indonesia have had devastating effects on the microfinance industries in those countries. Whatever the emergency or the country, the effects are the same: higher costs, liquidity problems, and loss of assets. MFIs with risk management plans in place before the emergency are more likely to survive, remain stable, continue serving their clients, and even prosper.

Risk Categories

The most common risks can be included in three categories: financial, operational, and strategic. In addition, risks are either internal or external to the institution. Internal risks are largely within the MFI's control—related to operational systems and management decisions. External risks are largely outside the MFI's control. Table 1.1 illustrates the risks an MFI might confront.[2]

Because an MFI's loan portfolio is its most valuable asset, the financial risks—credit, market, and liquidity—are of greatest concern. Financial risks begin with the possibility that a borrower may not pay the loan on time with interest (credit risk). They include the possibility that the MFI might lose a significant part of the value of its loan portfolio as a result of an economic downturn, hyperinflation, and other externally generated causes (market risk). Financial risk can also include changes in interest rates of government lending programs (as in Bolivia and the República Bolivariana de Venezuela) or the possible enforcement of old usury laws (as in several Latin American countries). Market risks include lower prices for borrowers' products and services, which could directly affect their ability or willingness to repay an outstanding loan.

---

1. This chapter is based on the December 2006 dialogue with Rochus Mommartz (Boulder Institute of Microfinance), Hans Dellien (Women's World Banking), and Fernando Fernández (Development Alternatives Inc.).
2. Because of the different ways of understanding risk, an institution might organize risks differently from the presentation in table 1.1. See, for example, van Greuning and Bratanovic (2000: 257–60).

Table 1.1 **Urban Risk Categories**

Risk Category	Subcategories	Specific risks
Financial risks	Credit	Loan portfolio (internal)
		Interest rate (internal or external)
		Loan enforcement practices (internal)
		Loan rescheduling and refinancing practices (internal)
	Market	Prices (external)
		Markets (external)
		Exchange rate (currency) (external)
		Value chain (external)
	Liquidity (internal)	Cashflow management issues (internal)
Operational risks	Transaction (internal)	
	Fraud and Integrity (internal)	Branch-level authority limits on lending
	Technological (internal)	Information and technology
	Human Resources (internal)	Staff training Operational manuals
	Legal and Compliance (internal)	Operational audits, financial audits
	Environmental (external)	Specific environmental impacts
Strategic risks	Performance (internal)	Generating profits and returns on assets and on equity to attract investors
	External Business (external)	New financial sector laws
	Reputational (external)	Competitive pressures (existing, new actors)
	Governance (internal)[a]	Changes in regulatory practices (licensing and reporting requirements) (external) Lack of board consistency and direction (internal)
	Country (external)	Relationships with donors and government programs (external)
Producer risks	Experience	
	Technology	
	Management Ability	

Note: This table was developed by the authors and is based on a variety of sources. See, for example, Fernández (2006) and Steinwand (2000). See also Deutsche Gesellschaft für Technische Zusammenarbeit, http://www.gtz.de/en/.

a. See chapter 2 of this volume.

Given the rapid pace at which demand for funds can grow, MFIs should be particularly aware of liquidity risk—the lack or shortage of funds for current and future expenses or loans. Liquidity risk can result from an overly aggressive lending strategy, low levels of on-time payment, seasonal variations of demand (such as the Christmas season or the planting and harvest cycle), or unanticipated expenses.

To prepare for these risks, MFIs usually hold in reserve between 15 and 20 percent of assets in cash and in short-term assets. Compared to the holdings of other financial institutions (which maintain liquidity of between 5 percent and 10 percent), this reserve is high, but it allows for a great degree of short-term flexibility.

A recent review of a Honduran MFI illustrates the increased risk of an overly aggressive lending strategy. Over time, the MFI had invested 93 percent of its assets in the loan portfolio, leaving only 7 percent in cash and in short-term assets. As a result, to meet its financial obligations, the MFI had to decide whether to liquidate its assets or obtain more expensive funding.

Like liquidity risks, operational risks are within the MFI's control. They include the risk of loss through faulty internal processes, poorly trained personnel, and inadequate information systems. Operational manuals, clear terms of reference for key positions, loan officer rotation, checks and balances systems (such as separation of certain responsibilities), and internal and external audits all contribute to sound operational systems, and they help to manage those risks.

Strategic risks include long-term choices and changes in the business environment. Strategic risks can include inappropriate business strategies, introduction of riskier products, branch location decisions, choice of strategic alliances, and changes in market structure (caused by new entrants, new laws, and new regulations).

Management of the Biggest Risks

The type of MFI can affect the institution's risk level.[3] State-owned banks engaged in microlending, for example, can be subject to political pressures to forgive debt or divert credit, both of which can result in poor loan recovery rates. Private commercial banks that undertake microfinance pilots may be limited by regulatory norms, such as the prohibition on lending without adequate collateral. However, specialized microfinance banks are better equipped to manage the risks involved in lending to informal sector businesses.

Membership-based MFIs develop close and long-term relationships with clients. Financial cooperatives (credit unions and savings and loans cooperatives) provide both savings and credit to members. Multipurpose cooperatives provide inputs, marketing, transportation, and other services that make it easier for members to sell their products and to repay their loans on time. Those complementary services tighten the bond between individual members and the MFI. Community-based financial organizations (such as village banks and self-help groups) also know their members intimately and can respond to needs while managing the accompanying risks.

Regardless of the type of institution, the nature of microfinance itself often increases certain risks faced by financial institutions, while offering innovative means of dealing with them. The biggest risks include (1) client selection, (2) product risk, (3) portfolio composition, and (4) loan processing and information management.

Client selection risk

Adverse client selection occurs when the MFI agrees to loan funds to a risky client because of incomplete information. Adverse selection can lead to a decline in the quality of the portfolio because the high-risk clients cannot or will not repay the loans. Adverse selection can also lead to moral hazard, which is the possibility that clients who know that they are fully protected from risk will act less responsibly and more speculatively than if they were fully exposed to the consequences of risk taking. For this reason, well-publicized guarantee funds often run into serious problems in the early stages; they can attract clients speculating in high-risk ventures.

When the MFI enforces loan repayment, it demonstrates to potential clients that the loan contract is a serious commitment of future resources and that there are specific consequences for failure to repay a loan. Easy restructuring and refinancing policies make it difficult for good loan officers to enforce contracts with good clients. After all, why shouldn't good clients get the same lenient treatment as poor performers? However, additional charges and higher interest rates when loans are restructured improve the incentive to

---

3. For more detailed information on the specific risks of each type of microfinance service provider, see Ritchie (2007: 43–48).

repay on time. The penalties for late payment or nonpayment should be transparent, credible, and enforceable—while rewards, such as interest rate rebates for perfect performance, should also be clear.

To ensure portfolio quality, the internal control or risk assessment unit should define risks, establish credit limits and selection criteria, and learn to recognize early signs of trouble. For example, a credit information system can be constructed to identify the characteristics of poor performers and to lower the risk to the MFI over time. This system will promote a sound credit culture.

Product risk

Using experiences, demand studies, and other techniques, the MFI management team designs credit, savings, and other financial products. Every design choice, no matter how small, can create additional risks. Key elements of the design include

- Maximum and minimum loan amount
- Grace period
- Loan maturity
- Effective interest rate
- Payment schedule (monthly or seasonal payments)
- Collateral requirements
- Currency of the loan

The wrong product design choices can lead to disaster because they do not match the local culture and limitations of the MFI's clients. For example, loans that are too large can lead to overindebtedness. Loans that are too small can make it difficult for the borrower to meet operational expenses. Moreover, a long grace period may increase the risk of loan default, because there is no early indication of the client's ability or willingness to repay on time. If long-term loans dominate the portfolio, the MFI could experience a loss in the event of a sudden spike in inflation.

Lending in a foreign currency can be popular with clients because it allows them to import machinery more easily. However, the foreign exchange risk exposure can hurt the MFI's financial position if the foreign currency strengthens. In 2001, the Superintendency of Banks in Peru was concerned about the foreign currency mismatch for the Cajas Municipales de Ahorro y Crédito system. The portfolio—equivalent to 40 percent of foreign currency liabilities—left the MFIs vulnerable to a relative appreciation of the dollar. As the MFIs became aware of the currency risk, they began to monitor their currency exposure and adjusted the asset and liability sides of the balance sheet. By 2004, the foreign currency portfolio had reached more than 70 percent of the liabilities in dollars, a more manageable currency match.

The MFI may also include the "rules of the game" such as group requirements (meetings), participation in technical training, or forced savings (also known as compensatory balances). However, the MFI should consider each requirement's potential impact on the client's ability to pay and its own financial health. The MFI can reduce the risks by offering loan products designed to reflect the client's preferences, cashflow profiles and ability to repay, and seasonal and other opportunities or risks. For savings, the product can be based on the saver's preferences and seasonal excess liquidity holdings. However, if savings and loan products are based on the cashflow, liquidity, and other needs of the MFI, risks are very likely to increase. For instance, forced savings represent short-term liquidity and a kind of collateral to the MFI. However, forced savings take working capital out of the microbusiness and can increase the likelihood of late payment or nonpayment.

Portfolio composition

The types of loans in the MFI's portfolio can create or balance the risks inherent in lending money to informal businesses. Understanding the risks should lead to adequate loan loss provisions and reserves. Such reserves are a useful mechanism in risk management. For instance, a portfolio consisting of small short-term loans to rural borrowers can be sensitive to droughts, crop and animal diseases, floods, and hurricane winds. Urban transportation strikes, protests, and flooding from heavy rains are examples of urban portfolio risks. In both cases, inadequate management of overdue loans can put the MFI at risk.

Maintaining adequate loan loss provisions will permit the institution to cover the likely losses. This maintenance is commonly achieved by building reserves based on the length of time a payment is overdue. For instance, an MFI may set up a reserve equal to 25 percent of loan balances with an overdue payment of 30 to 60 days; 50 percent of loan balances with an overdue payment of 61 to 90 days; and 100 percent of those with an overdue payment of more than 90 days. Finally, write-off policies play a complementary role to loan loss provisioning and reserves; a common practice is to write off loans more than 180 days past due.

Loan processing and information management

Another source of risk includes the processes, practices, and information systems used to track the loan portfolio. A management information system tracks individuals, groups, sectors, and branches to identify quickly any threats to strong portfolio performance. The German microfinance management firm Internationale Projekt Consult GmbH has developed the ProCredit banking system, a standardized management information system that provides daily delinquency reports to loan officers. This system emphasizes the importance of timely follow-up and rewards loan officers with bonuses based on the performance of their loan portfolio.[4]

Finally, other internally and externally determined risk factors affect an MFI's ability to manage the client development and loan collection processes. The internally determined risk factors include hiring policies, incentive systems, operating policies and procedures, employee evaluations, management information systems and reports, asset and liability management, currency management (hedging), and internal controls and audits. External factors are the accessibility and usefulness of credit bureaus, the ease of collateral valuation and recovery (when necessary), competitive pressures, and the availability of insurance for clients.[5]

Producer Risks

The producer risks that urban microbusinesses represent are largely the result of the businesses' informal operations. Microbusinesses usually fail to diversify their sources for key components and raw materials, relying instead on a few local suppliers. Because they often work out of home-based workshops, they rarely have formal warehouses to store raw materials, work in progress, and finished products. Those businesses also rely heavily in many cases on neighborhood clients, rather than developing long-lasting relationships with institutional clients. Their scale of operations is very limited, often making it difficult to meet the demands of schools, universities, and hospitals. Many microbusinesses use outdated designs and substandard materials, which limit their ability to find clients. They can also be affected by general strikes, which paralyze urban markets with little

4. See Internationale Projekt Consult GmbH, http://www.ipcgmbh.com/.
5. See chapter 4 of this volume for a discussion of microinsurance.

warning. Finally, some cannot provide enough character references and transparent records to compensate for the lack of physical collateral.

Additional Risks for MFIs with Rural Portfolios

MFIs serving rural clientele confront risks related to the natural resource base, the environment, and the cycles and risks of agricultural production. Many experts encourage urban MFIs to expand into the countryside and meet the challenges of the credit-hungry rural zones. MFIs already serving rural areas are aware of the challenges—yet they often fail to reach scale, control costs, or effectively enforce contracts when necessary. Table 1.2 lists the risks associated with rural areas.[6]

Table 1.2 **Rural Risk Categories**

Market risks	Price volatility
	Irregular access to markets
	Poor infrastructure
	Inadequate information
Production risks	Land productivity
	Pests
	Disease
	Postharvest risks
Producer risks	Experience
	Technology
	Management ability
Climate risks	Drought
	Flood
	Wind
	Freeze
	Hail
	Heat Wave
Source: Authors.	

Market risks

Market risks specific to rural lending include changes in interest rates, exchange rates, prices for inputs and outputs, and relationships between key actors in value chains. To manage exposure to these risks, the microbusiness operator and the MFI focus on those factors they can control. For example, an MFI with a rural client base can link its borrowers to regularly updated databases on input and output prices. An MFI can also promote strategic relationships among its clients, super markets, agro-industry buyers, and exporters. International buyers are eager to build direct links to producer associations in Latin America—as the networks developed by the Starbucks, Home Depot, and Whole Foods chains have done. With the Calvert Foundation, Starbucks provided a US$1 million loan for onlending to small coffee farmers and cooperatives in Costa

---

6. See chapter 7 of this volume for a discussion of climate risks.

Rica, Mexico, and Nicaragua.[7] In Guatemala, for instance, the national coffee growers' association Anacafé provides updated prices for different types of coffee to more than 100,000 coffee producers. This timely market information helps producers to sell at the most advantageous time.[8]

New market relationships come with new challenges. For those new links to become permanent, urban microbusinesses and farmers alike must show that they can meet standards for product design, handling, packaging, labeling, and timely delivery. With the appropriate technical assistance, the small producer can develop a production and marketing plan to meet the new demand. Although it is not the MFI's direct responsibility to build such links, the advantages can include a growing client base that has assured markets awaiting their products and that will contribute to a healthier loan portfolio over time.

Production risks

From seed selection and warehousing to transport and final sales, microbusinesses confront a variety of production risks. To ensure reasonable risks, the MFI needs to develop a profile of the typical producer and the agricultural region. The profile will include

- Size of the cultivated area
- Crops produced in each season
- Number of growing seasons per year
- Regional average, maximum, and minimum productivity
- Production systems and level of technology
- Local warehousing issues
- Sales channels

With this deeper understanding of the region's producers and the environment in which they work, the MFI should collaborate with agricultural and technology transfer agencies to ensure adequate levels of capacity and technology. Subsector analysis, which offers maps of the key production and market relationships, can be a useful tool to identify risks and opportunities for high-impact technology innovations.

Producer risks

Rural microbusinesses are largely informal operations and represent a significant source of risk for the MFIs. Rural clients are often dispersed, increasing the costs of reaching them and enforcing loan contracts. Rural producers often have a subsistence mentality, rather than the profit maximization goal of a business. Their yields can be very low, since the rural producers frequently depend on traditional technologies, local seeds, and low-quality fertilizers. They tend not to diversify the source of inputs and are, therefore, vulnerable to sudden price increases and availability problems. Postharvest losses can compound the low productivity of the rural producer, with losses often amounting from 10 to 20 percent of total production. Finally, like their urban counterparts, most rural microbusinesses cannot provide sufficient character references and transparent records to compensate for the lack of physical collateral.

---

7. See Calvert Foundation, http://www.calvertfoundation.org/.
8. See Anacafé, http://www.anacafe.org/.

Development of a Risk Management System

To prepare for unexpected events and their costs, an MFI can identify and prepare for the most common and expensive risks. All financial institutions—large or small, regulated or unregulated—should design a risk management system that is based on the institution's particular needs, clients, products, legal status, and internal capacity.

For example, an MFI with a large share of loans in animal husbandry should prepare for a sudden drop in demand for its clients' products in local markets. A small rural MFI working with solidarity and communal groups—and providing credit only—should develop a risk management plan to deal with overdue loans, liquidity management, and fixed asset security. However, an urban-based regulated MFI, with a larger number and variety of financial products, is subject to the norms and procedures of a government supervisory institution. Its risk management system will have different goals and strategies. In addition, the Basel II accords (see box 1.1) serve as an international standard for capital requirements to balance the risks inherent in microfinance.

Box 1.1 Basel Committee: International Standards and Practices for Risk Management

Supervisor and regulators play an important role in financial institution risk management, using the international standards and definitions codified by the Basel Committee in 2005. The system protects creditor and savers in regulated financial institutions by ensuring capital adequacy. Capital adequacy is a key measure of the financial institution's ability to withstand shocks and reflects sound management of resources. In addition, an ongoing evaluation of capital adequacy protects against financial sector instability, a breakdown in payments systems, and the risk of international contagion effects. Basel I set the international standard by defining capital adequacy in terms of risk-weighted assets. Basel II reinforced the standard by introducing risk-based supervision practices.

Do the Basel requirements affect MFIs? When microfinance is a business line of a large regulated financial institution, the national supervisors take microfinance into account as part of an integrated review of the institution's risk management performance. However, for specialized, smaller MFIs, Basel standards are unlikely to be applied. This deviation is due to the MFI's small share of financial sector assets, the lack of complex operations, and the absence of significant interactions with international markets. Finally, MFIs are typically well capitalized. Very few cases of corrective action have been taken. If leverage should increase significantly, Basel standards could be applied using the risk-weighted approach and risk-based supervision requirements. This occurrence would have implications for both MFIs and their clients in the form of higher costs and higher interest rates.

Source: Adapted by authors from Imboden (2005). See: www.microfinancegateway.org/p/site/m/library/.

An MFI that develops an early warning system can respond before the risks become larger and more costly. The early warning system will evolve with the changing risks confronting the institution, thereby protecting its short-term solvency and long-term viability (see Steinwand 2000).[9] The management team is responsible for periodically assessing the MFI's exposure to risk and determining its risk management strategy. For instance, the assessment will be based on the institution's particular circumstances—the legal and regulatory context, inflation, the sources of funds (such as the mix of loans and grants, grace period, rates of interest, repayment terms), client location (rural or urban) and activities (agriculture, animal husbandry, commerce, services or production).

---

9. See also Deutsche Gesellschaft für Technische Zusammenarbeit, http://www.gtz.de/en/.

Steps in Risk Management

Table 1.3 describes the steps in risk management. The first step is to identify the institution's unique risk profile by analyzing the institution's goals, needs, costs, and profitability. This step identifies the institution's social and financial goals. It also assesses whether the operation is profitable and whether costs are adequately covered. In the second step, the MFI defines those unexpected events, or risks, that are most likely to occur and most important to manage. This process can be based on recent trends and experiences of other MFIs, as well as on potential political and economic changes. Management should focus on the top five internal and external risks. Using this analysis, in the third step, the MFI sets exposure limits for each line of business, for example, the percentage of total loans to a particular sector or a region or the percentage of loans delinquent beyond 30 days. In the fourth step, once a limit has been passed, the institution implements its risk analysis and control activities. Finally, the MFI adjusts the risk management system periodically—revising its risk profile and operational systems, as the political and business environments change over time.

Table 1.3 **Steps in Risk Management**

Step	Actions
Identify risk profile, in delivery of financial services.	Identify • Goals, needs, costs, and profitability • Internal risks • External risks
Define most important risks (reviewed annually by management).	Select • Top 5 internal risks • Top 5 external risks
Set limits.	Set • Acceptable delays • Acceptable costs • Acceptable level of losses • Acceptable risks at the branch level • Risk levels measured in other ways
Implement analysis and control system of regular checks and balances.	Implement and monitor processes, reviews, and internal audits—when limits are passed.
Manage and monitor risks.	Look for risk patterns, and address them strategically and operationally.
Source: Adapted by authors from Mommartz (2006).	

For each risk category—internal or external—the successful MFI assesses the possible effects on its loan portfolio and policies. The portfolio includes all the outstanding loans, whether they are timely or overdue. The loans may be of different size and character (individual or group) and to different productive sectors. According to its mission and strategy, the MFI may have made preferential loans to women or productive sectors. In addition, its interest rates may or may not be competitive. Finally, the MFI's holdings in other currencies will subject the portfolio to changes in the exchange rate. The portfolio assessment will identify risks and help management to establish a balanced mix of loans. The following criteria will assist in developing the assessment:

- Sectors to be served
- Training level of the staff
- Geographic coverage and depth
- Level of tolerance for delayed payments

- Products to be provided the various markets or niches
- Market niches—based on the mission statement and management and the board of directors

Internal tools and externally provided services help to measure these risks. Table 1.4 and box 1.2 describe the risk analysis tools used by Shorebank Advisory Services and the CAMEL (Capital Adequacy, Asset Quality, Management, Earnings, and Liquidity Management) approach used by ACCIÓN International, respectively. Other specialized external ratings services that focus on MFIs include Microfinanzas, Planet Finance, and Microrate. Microfinance Information Exchange provides an international rating service. The Consultative Group to Assist the Poor offers a risk identification tool in its appraisal handbook.[10]

Table 1.4 **Shorebank Advisory Services (USA) Credit Risk Grading System**

General Risk	Credit risk grade	Description
Low risk	Grade 1 – Excellent Grade 2 – Good Grade 3 – Satisfactory	Loans develop according to projections or better, and no problems with repayment have ever occurred or are anticipated.
Potential risk	Grade 4 – Watch List	Loans show deviations from the project's business development scenario, and problems with repayments can be anticipated.
High risk	Grade 5 – Substandard Grade 6 – Doubtful Grade 7 – Loss	Loans have different terms of delinquency, and they are associated with different probabilities of being fully repaid. The longer the loan is delinquent, the less likely it is that the balance would ever be repaid in full.

Source: Adapted by the authors from the Palestinian Network, Fact Sheet 5, "Risk Management and the Credit Risk Grading System," http://www.shorebankcorp.com/bins/site/templates/default.asp.

---

10. For more information, see Microfinanzas, http://www.microfinanzas.org/; Planet Finance, http://us.planetfinance.org/; Microrate, http://www.microrate.com/; The Microfinance Information Exchange, http://www.themix.org/; The Microfinance Information Exchange Market, http://www.mixmarket.org/; and Consultative Group to Assist the Poor, http://www.cgap.org/p/site/c/.

Box 1.2 Risk Measurement Systems

North American bank regulators first adopted the CAMEL methodology to evaluate the financial and managerial soundness of U.S. commercial lending institutions. The CAMEL reviews and rates five areas of financial and managerial performance:

- Capital Adequacy
- Asset Quality
- Management
- Earnings
- Liquidity Management

Using the original CAMEL's conceptual framework, ACCIÓN International developed its own instrument. The ACCIÓN CAMEL reviews the same five areas, but the indicators and ratings reflect the challenges and conditions of the microfinance industry. The methodology requires the MFI to provide the following information:

- Financial statements
- Budgets and cashflow projections
- Portfolio aging schedules
- Funding sources
- Information about the board of directors
- Operations and staffing
- Macroeconomic information

The ACCIÓN CAMEL performs the following adjustments: (1) loan loss provision, (2) loan write-offs, (3) explicit and implicit subsidies, (4) effects of inflation, and (5) accrued interest income. The ACCIÓN CAMEL analyzes and rates 21 key indicators, with each indicator given an individual weighting. The final composite rating is a number on a scale of zero to five, with five as the measure of excellence. This numerical rating corresponds to an alphabetical rating (AAA, AA, A, BBB, BB, B, C, D, and unrated).

Source: Global Development Research Center, http://www.gdrc.org/.

Approaches to Managing Risks

Successful MFIs employ several risk management strategies. They develop strong internal information systems to allow managers to understand and mitigate the risks related to liquidity, internal fraud, and new product development. They ensure better information on the cashflow, productivity, and other characteristics. Their credit management systems keep a watchful eye on portfolio quality issues, allowing for swift responses to willful default. They recognize the value of microinsurance to protect borrowers from insurable risks (see chapter 4 of this volume for microinsurance). They consistently enforce the loan contract. Finally, their incentives for loan officers are linked directly to portfolio performance.

In addition to these general approaches, specific recommendations exist for the special conditions in rural finance markets. Greater information on borrowers, crop cycles, productivity levels, and market cycles can reduce the risks of serving rural clients and provide a sound basis for product design. Using such information, MFIs can design the loan product's specific characteristics (including any grace period, the repayment schedule, installment or lump sum payments, and the effective interest rate) to accommodate price volatility and the client's cashflow.

To address the issue of low crop productivity, the MFI can help microbusinesses form an alliance with business service providers—an agricultural technology institute, for example. This relationship can provide farmers (MFI clients) with access to improved seeds and pesticides, recent developments in land management techniques and production technologies, and improved postharvest practices. It would also help the clients move from traditional to more commercially oriented production and business practices.

Finally, to improve access to clients in dispersed rural settlements, MFIs should take advantage of low-cost technologies such as mobile phone–based microfinance transactions or banking service correspondents (see chapter 8 of this volume on technologies).

Because risks are unavoidable, they must be managed. Risk management systems are, in effect, the wings needed before taking the leap of faith of lending to large numbers of informal microbusinesses. MFIs with effective risk management systems in place are far better prepared for the unexpected, and this preparation can be the difference between growth, stability, or bankruptcy. By instilling a culture of risk management throughout the institution, from the board of directors to loan officers and internal operations staff members, the MFI and its clients should be able to manage unexpected events—and even thrive.

References

Bradbury, Ray. Undated. http://www.brainyquote.com/quotes/authors/r/ray_bradbury.html.

Fernández, Fernando. 2006. *"La Gestión de Riesgos en Instituciones Microfinancieras: Una Perspectiva Rural."* Access to Rural Finance for Microenterprise Projects, Mexico, December 11.

Imboden, Kathryn. 2005. "Basel II and Microfinance: Exercising National Prerogatives." Women's World Banking. http://www.swwb.org.

Mommartz, Rochus. 2006. *"Introducción a la Gestión de Riesgos y su Contexto."* Paper presented at a workshop at the World Bank, Washington, DC, December 11.

Ritchie, Anne. 2007. "Community-based Financial Organizations: A Solution to Access in Remote Rural Areas?" Agriculture and Rural Development Discussion Paper 34, World Bank, Washington, DC.

Steinwand, Dirk. 2000. "A Risk Management Framework for Microfinance Institutions." MicroFinance Network prepared for Deutsche Gesellschaft für Technische Zusammenarbeit, Chicago, July. http://www.gtz.de/en/.

Van Greuning, Hennie, and Sonja Bratanovic. 2000. *Analyzing Banking Risk.* Washington, DC: World Bank.

Additional Sources

Dellien, Hans. 2006. *"Crédito Rural: Estrategias para mitigar los riesgos agropecuarios."* Paper presented at a workshop at the World Bank, Washington, DC, December 11.

Fernando, Maheshan R. 2005. "Managing Foreign Exchange Risk: The Search for Innovation to Lower Costs to Poor People." Microfinance Matters 12, United Nations Capital Development Fund. http://www.uncdf.org/english/microfinance/pubs/newsletter/pages/2005_05/news_managing.php.

Uva, Wen-feil L. 2004. "Managing Market Risks," Smart Marketing Newsletter, Cornell University, Department of Applied Economics and Management. Ithaca, NY, April. http://hortmgt.aem.cornell.edu/pdf/smart_marketing/uva4-04.pdf.

2 GOOD GOVERNANCE: MANAGING INTERNAL RISK

If words of command are not clear and distinct, if orders are not thoroughly understood, the general is to blame.

*Sun Tzu**

* *The Art of War by Sun Tzu: Special Edition,* trans. Lionel Giles (El Paso, TX: El Paso Norte, 2005).

Effective management is critical for a microfinance institution (MFI) to achieve long-term financial success and its social mission. MFIs must manage change and make difficult decisions with clarity and consistency of vision and mission. To be able to offer new products and services, successful MFIs must navigate changing laws and regulations, increasing competition, entrance of new types of competitors (for example, banks), and changes in technology, among other challenges. At the same time, they must deal with risk and vigilantly guard against fraud and loss of assets.

This chapter describes governance concepts as they apply to the microfinance sector. It begins with a brief discussion of MFI owners and their effect on MFI governance. It then addresses the board and the board's pivotal role in sound MFI governance, outlining general best practices in MFI board operation. Finally, it includes a governance self-evaluation tool (see annex) and a short reference list of relevant resources.[1]

The role of governance may be defined broadly as the system of people and processes through which an organization maintains its focus and ensures institutional success. It includes the checks and balances needed to "manage managers." Ultimately, good governance seeks

- To uphold the organization's goals and mission
- To guide the organization's major strategic direction
- To maintain an organization's health over time and to mitigate risks
- To ensure accountability throughout the organization[2]

Despite the availability of resources that detail sound corporate and nonprofit governance, a 2008 survey found quality of governance to be the second-greatest risk facing MFIs during times of rapid change. The survey revealed that many in the sector have strong doubts that many MFIs have the ability to adapt to new demands and still retain their social objectives.[3]

Ownership, Legal Form, and Their Impact on Governance[4]

Governance of any institution is closely related to its ownership. The ownership structure has a significant effect on board structure, its effectiveness, and the risks it faces. Owners provide or control the institution's funds or capital and are interested in the institutional mission and results. Therefore, they want enough influence to ensure adequate accountability through institutional governance.

Different types of owners have particular sets of concerns, all of which tend to be closely linked to what the owner is hoping to gain from the investment. Because most MFI investors have financial and nonfinancial goals and priorities, they frequently use a "double bottom line" system, which balances financial goals with a social mission, or a "triple bottom line" system, which adds environmental concerns: thus, they can evaluate the MFI's success. Some owners are more sensitive to loss of financial or physical assets; others, to loss of reputation, developmental goals, or institutional mission.

---

1. This chapter is based on the April 2007 dialogue with presentations by Todd Farrington (ACCIÓN International), Tillman Bruett (Alternative Credit Technologies LLC), and Juan Manuel Díaz Parrondo (Instituto Dominicano de Desarrollo Integral). Tillman Bruett was primarily responsible for this chapter, using the presentations, additional interviews, and research. He also developed the good governance instrument presented at the end of the chapter.
2. Council of Microfinance Equity Funds (2005), http://cmef.com/governancefinal.pdf.
3. Centre for the Study of Financial Innovation (2008), http://cmef.com/CMEF5-BananaSkins.pdf.
4. This discussion of ownership structure draws heavily from Otero (2001).

An institution's legal form also determines many aspects of its governance. Good governance is a challenge for all types of organization—from small nongovernmental organizations (NGOs) to large corporations. MFIs face most of the governance challenges of banks and financial institutions and some that are particular to socially oriented businesses. First, many MFIs are nonprofit entities or are owned by nonprofit entities and often have an unclear ownership structure. Second, the growth in assets and clients frequently leads to a change in an MFI's legal form or status requiring an evolution of its governance: from an NGO to a shareholder-owned institution, from a nonregulated to a regulated MFI. Finally, the legal and regulatory framework in which MFIs operate is dynamic and often either inadequate or excessively complicated. As a result, no one governance structure is universally applicable to all MFIs at all times. Good governance must be relevant for an MFI's particular situation and stage of development. It should also anticipate the next stage of development.

NGOs

In Latin America, NGOs continue to play a significant role as MFI owners and as operators. In most cases, donors—private foundations, governments, international aid agencies, or individuals—provide the bulk of capital to start and sustain the NGO. Because NGOs are nonprofit organizations with no real owners, the founders cannot lay claim to the organization's financial and physical assets.

This lack of specific owners makes it difficult to identify the person or institution to whom the board is accountable or for whom it acts as a fiduciary. In this case, the board is accountable first and foremost to the institutional mission as it is defined, approved, and understood by the various stakeholders, including those donors and agencies that have funded the NGO.

A common governance risk associated with NGO ownership (particularly where the NGO is the sole or majority shareholder) is the concentration of power in the hands of one person or a few people, usually the founders. At the same time, management may depend on the MFI for its livelihood. Those who provide financial support may lack the time, interest, or ability to adequately oversee the MFI. This may lead to management operating the MFI for the primary benefit of management. This risk is avoidable. Numerous MFIs have diligent and capable NGO board members who value their reputation and have strongly identified with and protected the institutional mission. The key is to understand the motivation and what is at stake for the MFI's leaders.

Private Investors

The challenge with private investors is to ensure that their concerns are adequately addressed and evenly balanced with the interests of other investors and stakeholders. Because they have something to lose (or gain), private investors tend to be active board members (see box 2.1). Private investors in microfinance may be divided between two types of owners: profit seekers and patient capitalists. Profit seekers are primarily interested in making a high return on their investment, attracted by the impressive financial results that some MFIs have achieved. Institutional mission is not an overriding concern for this group of investors, and there is a temptation to forgo longer-term objectives and sustainability for short-term profits. They require an exit strategy to ensure that they can take out profits in the near to medium term. Patient investors are motivated by long-term return on their investment and a sense of their own social responsibility. They generally support the institutional mission and are motivated to protect the financial health of the organization as the basis for future returns.

Box 2.1 Investors as Board Members

The Council of Microfinance Equity Funds surveyed MFIs and funders to determine the main concerns related to the participation of investors in governance. The concerns were as follows:

- Finding an appropriate balance between management and board; avoiding management capture of governance
- Determining appropriate management compensation
- Agreeing on an appropriate balance between social and financial goals
- Working effectively as minority shareholders, protecting minority shareholder rights, and forming effective shareholder groups
- Establishing commonly accepted standards for conflict of interest, board member compensation, use of independent directors, and so forth

Although many public investors prefer to keep a distance from board participation, an increasing number of private microfinance funds are not as reticent. They have tried to follow the ProFund example. ProFund was located regionally, giving it the opportunity to stay involved on a continuous, real-time basis, and was "universally appreciated" as a very engaged board member. In particular, it is well informed; in close contact with other board members, management, and other relevant parties; and willing and able to actively participate beyond formal board meetings as necessary. Private investors such as MicroVest Capital Management and Blue Orchard Finance, S.A., consider governance part of their investment strategy. In addition to ensuring adequate returns, such investors maintain a rigorous focus on the return of principal and fiduciary responsibilities of the board.

Source: Council of Microfinance Equity Funds 2005.

Government

Government funding for microfinance has a long history in Latin America, where national and local governments have created microfinance banks, savings banks, and other entities involved in microfinance. Governments often fund microfinance for a specific social or policy objective, such as combating poverty or fostering rural development. Three of the most common vehicles for channeling government money to microfinance include so-called state banks (entities that may be involved in retail lending), apex institutions (wholesale facilities that invest or lend in MFIs), and independent microfinance programs that may be administered by one or more government agencies (De Montesquiou, El-Zoghbi, and Latortue 2008).

Governments are mostly concerned with maintaining power and serving the population. In general, local government ownership models for microfinance have struggled because of politicized policies, targeted subsidized credits that distort markets, political interference in operations, and corruption. However, there are a few examples of publicly owned MFIs that perform well, such as the municipally owned Cajas Municipales de Ahorro y Crédito (CMACs) of Peru. Those CMACs, while subject to regulation by the Banking Superintendency, have financial and administrative autonomy. Their institutional structure is rigidly defined by legislation to ensure that each CMAC is an economically and politically independent organization. CMACs are governed by separate boards comprising local representatives, including, the private sector. Each CMAC reports to a federation that monitors performance and conducts internal auditing.

External Public Entities and Aid Agencies

External public entities include bilateral donor agencies and multilateral agencies (for example, the World Bank and the Corporación Andina de Fomento, among others), and public and international financial institutions (the International Finance Corporation, part of the World Bank). External public entities invest in MFIs primarily because of the social and economic benefits they hope to achieve, such as increased employment and income levels or promotion of solutions to social and economic problems. Donors may also have political concerns based on their relationship with the host country. In general, those institutions do not play an active governance role. Their policies usually require them to take a minority stake and often preclude their participation in governance. They are most concerned with avoiding losses and the consequent damage to their reputation or credit rating. Moreover, the public entities' internal structures and operating procedures can limit their contribution to good governance. Turnover among agency personnel, lack of microfinance expertise, and lack of time or budget to focus on governance issues are common problems.

Microfinance Investment Vehicles

A relatively new type of financial intermediary that mobilizes funds from public and private funders and channels them to MFIs is called a microfinance investment vehicle (MIV). While MIVs have been funding MFIs for more than a decade, their growth in recent years has been explosive—in 2005 alone, it is estimated that the combined MIV portfolio nearly doubled to US$1 billion by year's end (MicroRate 2006). According to a geographic investment analysis, 56 percent of this investment was done in Latin America and the Caribbean. The MIVs' primary concern is to recover their principal with a small return. Those funds are usually regional, closer to the MFI than are multilateral or international funders. The MIVs often allocate experienced staff members and resources to monitor the performance of the MFI. They are often able to provide input into key board decisions.

MFIs in Transformation

As an institution transforms from a nonprofit ownership structure to a for-profit structure, governance must also change. This usually means transitioning from an institution dominated by a founder or social entrepreneur into a more professionally managed institution with broader ownership and a formal governance structure. Such a transition requires significant delegation of authority to management with a wider array of checks and balances (see box 2.2). The original board must share institutional control with incoming shareholders; must fund the transformation; and must adopt a new structure, bylaws, and agreements that safeguard the rights of the new owners.[5] This transition is a difficult process for boards, as it requires the original board members to give up control to entering investors. Those new entrants may not share the same charitable goals and social agenda, or at least may ask for equal emphasis to be placed on commercially oriented goals and concerns. It is also important to note that members of corporate boards can be sued; members of NGO boards, generally, cannot.

Becoming a deposit-taking institution places additional functional and legal responsibilities on the board. If an MFI becomes regulated, its board will become the official point of contact between regulators and the MFI. Regulations often dictate how MFI governance is to be carried out and specify the necessary committees and their functions. Regulators may have the right to approve board members and determine whether they are "fit and proper" and bring the requisite skills.

---

5. For an internationally recognized set of corporate governance standards and guidelines, including the rights of shareholders, equitable treatment of shareholders, and the responsibilities of the board, see OECD (2004).

Box 2.2 Questions to Assess the Implications of an MFI's Ownership Structure

The following questions should be used to assess an MFI's ownership structure:

- Do the owners have the necessary expertise to govern effectively?
- Do the owners have "deep pockets"—the financial resources to support the MFI's growth?
- Are the owners appropriately neutral or immune to political influence?
- Are the owners able to stay in for the "long haul" or are they interested in selling and turning over ownership to others?
- Do new investors bring necessary knowledge, skills, and personal qualities to the board? Do they share the mission of the organization?
- Is the ownership structure forward looking, anticipating the resources and skills needed for the future, not just for today?

Source: Adapted from Ledgerwood and White (2006).

The Board of Directors: Functional Responsibilities

Governance takes place within a broad context; however, the board of directors is the "pivot point" through which all players connect. The board is a group of individuals who are either elected or appointed by shareholders, stakeholders, or members and who work with MFI management to guide the MFI to achieve its vision and mission. The functional responsibilities of the board of directors can be categorized into four broad groups: fiduciary, strategic planning, supervision, and management development (Clarkson and Deck 1997).

Fiduciary

A fiduciary is a person to whom property or power is entrusted for the benefit of another. In the case of an MFI board, the fiduciary is entrusted with financial and physical assets and must ensure their appropriate use while maintaining their value. In some cases, the law may make the MFI's board members personally and legally liable. While maintaining the MFI's adherence to the institutional mission, a board of directors must protect and promote the solvency, liquidity, and financial performance of the organization. Fiduciaries are most effective when they are proactive and encourage management to create a process that identifies, assesses, and controls risks. Fiduciaries should also encourage management to ask difficult questions, and then make or approve strategic decisions that balance the potential costs or benefits of taking particular risks.

Strategic planning

The board plays an important role in the development of the MFI's long-term strategy, usually in the form of a strategic plan. The board considers the principal risks facing the MFI and approves plans presented by management. In keeping with its role to ensure financial and operational survival of the institution, the board must examine whether the institution has adequate resources to implement its strategies. It also approves key strategic decisions, such as the opening of new branches; the introduction of new products and services or the entering into alliances, partnerships, or contracts with other organizations. Additionally, the entire board or specific members may participate directly in strategy development sessions.[6]

---

6. For young institutions, fundraising to fulfill plans may also be part of the board's role.

In executing its strategic responsibilities, the board must keep in mind all of its stakeholders. It is accountable to the MFI and its shareholders—and has a duty to act in their best interests—but should also consider the interests of employees, creditors, customers, suppliers, and the local communities. Moreover, it should observe relevant environmental and social standards (OECD 2004) (see box 2.3).

Box 2.3 The Board and Social Performance Management

Nearly all MFIs have social goals: their very existence—at least in part—is to serve a social purpose. An MFI's social goals must be clearly expressed within its mission. "Mission drift" occurs when an MFI's focus on social issues is lost because its purpose is vague or is neglected in pursuit of other goals (such as profitability or growth). One key role of an MFI's board is to protect and balance social and financial goals and to guard against mission drift. This is no easy task.

Social performance management (SPM) is an institutionalized process that involves setting clear social objectives, monitoring and assessing progress toward their achievement, and using this information to improve overall organizational performance. SPM engages a wide spectrum of stakeholders into the MFI's operations, including board members.

The key reference in SPM within microfinance is the global action-research Imp-Act Programme, which has worked with more than 30 organizations worldwide to develop an overarching framework that promotes SPM as a core business function. The framework combines regular monitoring of client status, analysis and communication of findings, and corresponding adjustments to products or service delivery that will improve the MFI's program.

Source: Campion, Linder, and Knotts 2008.

Supervision

The board delegates operational and administrative responsibilities to the chief executive officer (CEO) and the management team. However, it is responsible for monitoring management's performance in executing approved plans and for evaluating their performance against planned goals and timelines. For this reason, and to judge management impartially, the board should resist involving itself in the MFI's management of daily operations. If it becomes a surrogate for the staff, it will fail in its supervisory capacity. In times of institutional crisis or succession of a CEO, a board may be required to assume temporary management. However, this role should be relinquished as soon as competent management is restored. Finally, the board should periodically evaluate its own performance and effectiveness (see box 2.4).

Box 2.4 **Evaluating Board Performance**

In theory, the board is responsible to institutional shareholders and ensures that management acts in accordance with shareholder wishes. In practice, both within microfinance and elsewhere, many boards become servants of the CEO or one dominant shareholder. Recent high-profile corporate scandals involving boards that failed to act in shareholders' best interests raise an important question: how can shareholders evaluate whether or not the board is doing its job?

There are no set guidelines for conducting a board assessment: each board formulates its own plans for evaluation. However, as with the evaluation of the CEO, board assessment must be done regularly and against preset, well-defined criteria. These criteria should be established in board policy. The key areas to evaluate are as follows:

1. Board and committee structure
    - Does the board as a whole or an individual committee have the staff, skills, and experience to tackle its current or expected problems?
    - Are more independent directors needed to ensure financial and legal survival of the institution?
    - Do the committees meet often enough to fulfill their duties?
    - Do the committees receive and process information in an efficient and effective manner?
    - Do the committees keep the board apprised of risks and uncertainty in their areas of expertise and responsibility?
    - Do potential conflicts of interest or personal issues exist that may disrupt the cohesiveness of the group?
    - How strong is group cohesiveness? If deficiencies exist, how do they hinder the performance of certain committees or the board as a whole?

2. The responsibilities of the board
    - Is the board evaluating the company's financial and operational performance appropriately, or should other measures (quantitative or qualitative) be used?
    - Is the CEO fulfilling his or her duties and providing solid leadership?
    - Has the board adequately assessed the growth potential of the company?
    - Can the board better address the needs and concerns of its stakeholders (both equity and debt)?

3. The physical process that boards use to conduct business
    - Does the board or any individual committee spend enough time on vital issues or areas that can enhance stakeholder value?
    - Is the board using all of the available tools and resources to come to a conclusion?
    - Is there good communication between the board and management?

Source: Adapted from Curtis (2007).

Management development

During the early stages of an MFI's development and the transitional periods that follow, the board must guarantee the survival of the organization. This responsibility means having the right people at the right time. For example, the board supervises the selection, evaluation, and compensation of the management team. This supervision includes anticipating and preparing for management succession. The board must ensure that the management team has the needed skills to handle current operations and take on new challenges. The best means to achieving this skill set is the continuous measurement of managers' performance and professional development.

The Board of Directors: Effective Structure

To carry out its duties effectively, the board must establish a formal, participatory structure in which its roles and responsibilities are clearly defined.[7] Some key considerations are discussed below.

Board size

Board size varies from institution to institution. The number of stakeholders involved and their investment in the MFI should determine the appropriate number of board members. In microfinance, boards normally range from between 5 and 25 members; boards with membership between 7 and 11 are the most common. Whatever its size, the board should be large enough to provide adequate staffing to complete the governance work, obtain the necessary funding, promote the institution, and ensure that a quorum regularly attends the meetings. However, the board should be small enough to make decisions efficiently and to develop a personal relationship of trust among members. An odd number of seats will help prevent tie votes (though consensus decision making is preferable).

The board chair

The person who is chair of the board, or board chair, is responsible for providing leadership, presiding over meetings, and guiding the disparate points of view of the board's membership to consensus. The board chair should regularly interact with the MFI's top management. This interaction should be transparent and adhere to appropriate segregation of duties to avoid the appearance of collusion or impropriety. To be effective, a board chair must possess a range of characteristics and skills. He or she should be "a good leader, navigator, planner, organizer, communicator, interpreter, confidant, liaison, conscience, caretaker and troubleshooter" (Oregon School Boards Association 2009).

The board chair and the CEO should not be the same person. While this has been a common practice in corporate governance in the United States, current views are veering from this practice. In the microfinance sector, this practice is now considered a warning sign that control of the institution may be too concentrated in one person (see box 2.5).

---

7. This discussion of setting up an effective board structure draws from the Council of Microfinance Equity Funds (2005).

Box 2.5 Some "Do's" and "Don'ts" for Boards

To maintain the appropriate independence of the board and management, some direction is provided as follows:

Do the following:
- Clearly define roles between management and the board.
- Separate the role of the board chair and the CEO.
- Maintain distance from daily operations by delegating authority for operations to management through the CEO.
- Set clear, measurable goals for management, and monitor performance against those goals.
- Supervise the selection, evaluation, and compensation of the senior management team.
- Use board committees (audit, finance, compensation, personnel, risk management, and so forth) to perform specific functions.
- Require that members follow basic codes of conduct to carry out roles and responsibilities in good faith.
- Make binding decisions as a group.
- Work to achieve board consensus.
- Require accurate, timely information in order to make good decisions.
- Rely on external audits, independent internal audit reports, and third-party evaluations to verify reporting accuracy.

Don't do the following:
- Form a board composed of friends of the CEO.
- Appoint the same person as both CEO and board chair.
- Allow management to occupy a major share of seats on the board.
- Exercise too much oversight of management and interfere with its work.
- Fail to meet regularly or meet in a pro-forma fashion.

Source: Compiled by Tillman Bruett.

Some duties of the board chair include the following:

- Serve as the chief nonexecutive officer (officer not involved in daily management) of the MFI.
- Chair meetings of the board according to agendas developed together with the CEO.
- Appoint all committee chairs within the board.
- Take an active role in recruiting board members.
- Oversee succession of board members.
- Serve ex officio on board committees and attend their meetings when possible.
- Evaluate the effectiveness of the board and its members, and ensure the board carries out its mandate.

Board committees

In well-functioning boards, most of the work occurs in committees. Committees meet before the full board meetings and discuss issues relevant to their specific mandate. They report any findings and progress to the full board. Committee meetings may be supported by written agendas and recorded minutes. Common board committees include the following:

- *The Audit Finance Committee* meets and works with internal and external auditors without the participation of management in an effort to understand issues of control and the veracity of accounting and financial statements. This committee is involved in selecting external auditors and in hiring and overseeing the work of the internal auditor.
- *The Compensation Personnel Committee* oversees the administration of human resources and the development of personnel policies and procedures. This committee ensures appropriate hiring of and compensation for the CEO and other top managers. The committee may also be responsible for evaluation of the CEO's performance.
- *The Risk Management and Investment Committee* examines issues of asset and liability management. This examination includes making sure that management is adequately monitoring and addressing portfolio risks, maturity mismatches, and currency risks, as well as the need for financial resources in the form of loans and equity investment. This committee may also address the MFI's compliance with legal, regulatory, and funder requirements, as well as the timeliness and completeness of reporting.

The role of the CEO

The CEO guides and supports the board's activities. As the MFI's top manager, the CEO has the advantage of having intimate knowledge of the institution's operations and performance. A primary function, therefore, is to ensure that the board has adequate information to make informed decisions in governance and oversight. The CEO's main responsibilities include the following:

- Articulate MFI strategy to the board, and assist members to review, modify, and approve the business plan.
- Supply and structure information and materials to the board meetings to facilitate board action and decision making.
- Provide timely and accurate financial and operational reports to the board and committee meetings to assist in monitoring performance and progress.
- In conjunction with the board, develop institutional performance indicators in line with the institutional mission and the triple bottom line.
- Attend all appropriate board and committee meetings, and be available to answer questions of board members prior to and during such meetings.
- Assist in selecting and orienting new board members.

The Board of Directors: Effective Processes

Board meetings

The purpose of the full board meeting is to exchange information and make key decisions. These meetings may be held quarterly or monthly (as mandated by government regulation or board bylaws) and should be structured to deal quickly with routine tasks to leave sufficient time for strategic issues. To allow board members time to read and prepare for the meeting, a board should develop a standard agenda with relevant materials that is distributed in advance (see box 2.6). A board secretary should be appointed to record detailed minutes of the meeting. During the meeting, the chair should guide the meeting according to the agenda and try to adhere to the meeting timetable, but also allow time for adequate discussion and input by members.

Most of a board's work occurs in committee meetings and is brought to the full board for discussion and final decision. In the interest of full transparency, board members should never discuss agenda items outside of the committee meeting or full board meeting. Board decisions should be taken by consensus whenever possible. Voting on issues may be necessary from time to time, but frequently resolving issues by vote may indicate that members are divided by vision or priorities.

Management reviews

The primary role and challenge of the board is to hold management accountable. There are formal means to do this during board meetings, committee meetings, and regular reporting, but boards should schedule an annual or semi-annual performance review of the CEO. Perhaps the most important role for the board is to establish transparent, fair, and measurable benchmarks for management's performance. These rules should be closely linked to the MFI's business plan, but should include elements that measure the CEO's effective management of staff, physical and financial resources, and management's demonstrated commitment to the institution's mission.

Box 2.6 Sample Board Meeting Agenda

1. Review of agenda and addition of new items
2. Review of previous meeting minutes
3. CEO's presentation of management report, including action items from previous meeting
4. Review of financial performance:
    a. Year-to-date performance versus plan
    b. Asset quality (loan portfolio and other investments)
    c. Key indicators (profitability, efficiency and productivity, and outreach)
    d. Credit exposure (by product, geography, and industry)
    e. Individual branch performance
5. Review of social performance versus plan
6. Management presentation on external environment
    a. Market
    b. Competition
    c. Funders
    d. Regulation
7. Compliance report
    a. Regulations
    b. Report on timeliness of external reporting
    c. Contract covenants and targets
8. Treasury report and risk management issues
    a. Budget update
    b. Liquidity and access to funds
    c. Asset/liability mismatches
9. Human resources update
10. Internal auditor presentation
11. Technology updates and other items
12. Identification and documentation of action items

Source: Ledgerwood and White 2006.

Information and disclosure

Board oversight quality is heavily dependent on the quality and timeliness of information supplied to members by the MFI's management. This dependence is closely tied to the quality of the MFI's management information systems, accounting personnel and practices, and internal controls systems. To avoid faulty decision making, the board should clearly understand what information it needs, what should and can be tracked regularly, and how the management information systems are able (or unable) to gather that information.

The board should be aware of the MFI's reporting requirements. A good starting point in designing a financial performance monitoring system, for example, is for the board to do an inventory of existing reporting requirements. The board should pay particular attention to how well management is using information to inform operations, make decisions, and propose new strategies. A list of common reports and information provided to board members includes the following:

- Financial and operating reports on a monthly or quarterly basis, including a set of carefully chosen indicators for tracking progress against financial goals, operational plans, and the MFI's social mission. These reports should give the board a complete and focused picture of progress regarding the triple bottom line.[8]
- A complete board information package for each monthly or quarterly meeting including (1) the current agenda, (2) minutes of the prior meeting, (3) management reports, (4) board committee reports, and (5) any additional information relevant to issues to be raised in the meeting.

Additionally, the board should use the following to verify reports it receives from management: independently audited financial statements, together with the auditor's management letter and any responses given by MFI management on a yearly basis, and internal audit reports as frequently as deemed necessary by the Audit Committee.

Training and development

Good governance must be developed over time. Effective boards undertake specific activities aimed at helping members to learn and grow in their ability to support and lead their MFI to the achievement of the institutional mission and objective (see box 2.7). Common training and improvement activities include

- Training sessions on best practices in microfinance and understanding of key financial and social indicators for measuring progress, which may involve internal MFI staff members or external experts
- Retreats to build relationships and consensus between board members regarding the balance of financial and social objectives
- Client visits to acquaint members with the MFI's operations, products, and services and also to gain the clients' perspective
- Self-evaluation on a yearly or biannual basis to measure effectiveness, identify strengths and weaknesses, and develop further strategies to improve board performance

---

8. For more information on financial performance monitoring from a board's perspective, see Bruett and Natilson (2002).

Box 2.7 A Case Study: The Dominican Integrated Development Institute

The Dominican Integrated Development Institute (Instituto Dominicano de Desarrollo Integral, or IDDI), founded in 1984, is a nonprofit institute focused on infrastructure, health, local development, and biosustainability. Its microcredit department was founded in 1990. Until 2002, management by the board of directors was largely absent, and this lack of leadership was reflected in IDDI's portfolio.

The board met only every two or three months, with little rotation of its membership and low levels of assistance. Its composition was not diverse, and it used very few sources of support. Moreover, the microfinance department was not institutionally independent. Although it could show good financial indicators and growth potential, few funds were available to meet demand. Worse, the systems of control and auditing were weak. As a result, IDDI had grown very little and its portfolio—with 90 percent equity—was out of balance.

The 2002 reforms addressed these weaknesses by improving management and oversight by the board of directors. Today, the board consists of seven members, each serving for two years. Board members meet every month. The assembly, with 21 members, meets yearly. The board has rededicated itself to preserving the mission and assets of the institute. To that end, it sponsored a CAMEL (Capital Adequacy, Asset Quality, Management, Earnings, and Liquidity Management) evaluation (see chapter 1 of this volume), separated the accounting and financial functions from the other departments, and restructured its debt-to-equity ratio. Finally, IDDI's microcredit center has grown by an outstanding 400 percent to US$2.5 million, 2,800 clients, and 14 employees.

Source: Compiled by Tillman Bruett.

Third-party reviews

Boards can benefit from a third-party review that includes an evaluation of the board itself. Reviews such as regulatory reviews or external audits may be legally. Others, such as rating reviews or internal evaluations, may be voluntary. A board should not hesitate to ask reviewers to consider its performance and activities. An experienced regulator, rater, or consultant can often identify the strengths and weaknesses of a board's structure, its monitoring procedures, and its activities and then make recommendations to improve board effectiveness. The following checklist presents an effective approach to board self-evaluation (Curtis 2007: 62):

- Get directors on board.
- Focus on group dynamics, such as committee and overall board performance. Be aware that peer evaluations can cause friction and disrupt board cohesiveness.
- Design the process internally.
- Do not overlook individual board member assessment.
- Focus on issues that will allow the board to do its job.
- Pay particular attention to
    - Staffing needs
    - Skill set of individual directors
    - Board members' ability to communicate with one another
    - Experience of individual board members
    - Potential conflicts of interest

- The board's ability to access accurate information and thereby enable it to assess future business opportunities
- The board's ability to communicate with management
- Consider the legal ramifications: Limit access to board evaluation results, and limit the paper trail.
- Generate actionable results: Focus on strengths and weaknesses. Use the information garnered to build team cohesiveness and improve decision making.

The Board of Directors: Member Selection and Participation

For development of an effective board, five critical considerations contribute directly to the board's performance and transparency: board member characteristics, board composition, the service period, conflict of interest policies, and compensation policies. Each of those is discussed next, with some specific good practices provided.

Necessary characteristics of board members

An effective MFI board needs members with a variety of skills. Board members should ideally possess an abundance of leadership characteristics and multiple technical skills (see table 2.1). Banking laws and regulations require that financial institution board members meet a "fit and proper" test. This term generally means that members should be of good moral character with no record of bankruptcy or criminal convictions and possess an appropriate level of experience. All board members should develop the capacity to analyze financial reports because each one assumes fiduciary responsibility on a personal level. Special attention should also be given to educate board members on risk management as it relates to MFIs.

Table 2.1 Recommended Characteristics and Background of a Board Member

Leadership Characteristics	Technical Background
• Commitment to the MFI's mission • Integrity and trustworthiness • Demonstrated success as a leader • Communication skills • Common sense and good judgment • Willingness to make the time commitment • Understanding of the personal commitment • Ability to work well with other board members	• Banking • Microfinance • Accounting • Law • Public relations • Marketing • Human resources • Entrepreneurial or business management • Community or social development • Information technology • Fundraising
Source: Author.	

Board composition

In new MFIs, board member selection is often based on a personal relationship with a dominant founder. Funders may request the authority to appoint board members as part of their investment agreement. As a result, management and other board members may be limited in their ability to influence the profile of investor-appointed board members. Important checks and balances are often disregarded when long-standing personal relationships prevent board members from effectively overseeing management activities. This type of board is not uncommon in the early stages of an organization, yet as the MFI grows and changes, those board members should cede control to individuals who are not constrained by this potential conflict of interest.

As the needs of the organization change and the membership of the board rotates, members should be recruited to match the organization's current and future needs. For example, if an MFI introduces microinsurance products, it may wish to invite a professional with experience in underwriting to join the board. In addition, cultural, ethnic, and gender diversity ensures that the board maintains a broad perspective. For example, the board of an MFI that serves female clients should seek to maintain significant female representation on its board.

Varying opinions exist regarding the inclusion of clients and employees on the board. One school of thought (associated with Continental Europe) maintains that employee representation is healthy, while another school of thought (more Anglo-American) maintains that staff participation blurs the line between the government, management, and staff. In addition, while the client's perspective is undoubtedly important to maintaining effective governance, the inclusion of clients on boards has not been particularly successful. Client representatives often lack the skills or broader perspective to participate in a meaningful way.

Service period and participation

The service period for board members should be sufficiently long to develop a strong leadership unit, but short enough to continually introduce new members with fresh perspectives and novel ideas. The typical board member commitment ranges from two to four years. Board member terms should be staggered to prevent a large, simultaneous replacement of directors; it is important to maintain a continuity of ideas and objectives on the board. Members who do not participate during a specific period or who fail to meet board standards should be removed. Also, the number of sequential service periods should be limited.

Letters of appointment and conflict of interest policies

Two useful tools to formalize the participation of board members include the letter of appointment and conflict of interest policies. The letter of appointment should include detailed information on expected responsibilities, expected time commitment, compensation structure, legal liabilities and obligations, codes of conduct for board members, and conflict of interest policies (see box 2.8).

Box 2.8 Responsibilities and Standards of Conduct for Board Members

Commitment to accountability, sometimes termed the fiduciary responsibility of board members, must infuse the performance of individual board members. Board members should act as follows:

- Know the mission, purpose, and goals of the MFI and its policies and programs.
- Understand the organization's strengths and weaknesses; a strategic role is to address these strengths and weaknesses.
- Prepare for, attend, and participate in board and committee meetings.
- Ask substantive questions; a key role of the board is to probe and to make policy decisions.
- Review and understand the MFI's financial statements and related information.
- Avoid making an uninformed judgment or policy decision. If information is inadequate, work with management to get the information needed.
- Represent the interests of the MFI as a whole, not those of any individual investor.
- Support the majority view once a decision is made.
- Maintain confidentiality.
- Maintain independence, objectivity, personal integrity, and ethical standards.
- Avoid conflicts of interest, inter-related transactions, insider lending, and nepotism.
- Meet personal disclosure requirements.

Source: Council of Microfinance Equity Funds 2005.

It is particularly important that the MFI board have clear policies relating to conflict of interests. Hidden or inappropriate relationships between board members and their institutions are one of the largest single causes of financial institutional demise. Even minor conflicts of interest can damage an MFI's internal trust or public image. What constitutes an unacceptable conflict of interest varies between countries and cultures, but certain key elements of a sound conflict-of-interest policy include

- No related lending to directors, their relatives, or businesses in which they have a stake
- Full disclosure of all conflicts and withdrawal of members from decision making on matters in which conflict exists
- Prohibition of business transactions between an institution and its board unless they are carried out on an arm's length basis with acceptable competition, market prices, and limits or special approval requirements

Board member compensation

There is some disagreement over compensation of MFI board members. Some people argue that directors who volunteer their time share the MFI's social commitment and serve MFIs with a strong sense of mission. Others believe that compensation is important to help attract skilled people to the board and motivate them to take their responsibilities seriously. One approach to compensation is to pay board members for their time spent working on board matters at a rate commensurate with senior level professionals and benchmarked against fees paid by similar organizations in the country. Many MFIs cover related expenses for board members who must travel to attend meetings.

Summary and Conclusions

Good governance is a challenge for all types of organization—including MFIs. Although no one governance structure is universally applicable to all MFIs, or even to the same MFI at different developmental stages, the board of directors is the pivot point that connects all concerned with good governance. A board consists of appointed or elected persons who represent institutional stakeholders and provide oversight and direction to managers of the institution.

A well-functioning board carefully attends to its fiduciary, strategic, supervisory, and management development roles. Much the board's work is achieved through committees, which prepare their work before board meetings. The board chair and the CEO play important roles in board activities, but neither should dominate the board. One person should not fill both of these roles at the same time.

Important characteristics of the board include its size, its composition, and the skills that each member brings to the board. Upon selection, board members should have their roles, duties, and responsibilities explained to them; a letter of appointment is a useful way to clearly communicate such information to new members. Codes of conduct for board members and conflict of interest policies are also necessary documents for guiding members in appropriate board behavior. The board should evaluate its effectiveness, as well as the effectiveness of its individual members, on a regular basis. Boards should also undertake development activities aimed at helping members and the collective to grow in ability and unity in successfully leading their institution to achieve its mission and objectives.

References

Bruett, Tillman, and Nancy Natilson. 2002. *Financial Performance Monitoring: A Guide for Board Members of Microfinance Institutions.* Washington, DC: The SEEP Network.

Campion, Anita, Chris Linder, and Katherine E. Knotts. 2008. *Putting the "Social" in Performance Management: A Practice-Based Guide for Microfinance.* Brighton, U.K.: Institute for Development Studies. http://www2.ids.ac.uk/impact/spm_practice_guide.pdf.

Centre for the Study of Financial Innovation. 2008. *Microfinance Banana Skins 2008: Risk in a Booming Industry.* http://cmef.com/CMEF5-BananaSkins.pdf.

Clarkson, Max, and Michael Deck. 1997. "Effective Governance for Microfinance Institutions." Focus Note 7, Consultative Group to Assist the Poor, Washington, DC.

Council of Microfinance Equity Funds. 2005. "The Practice of Corporate Governance in Shareholder-Owned Microfinance Institutions: Consensus Statement of the Council of Microfinance Equity Funds." http://cmef.com/governancefinal.pdf.

Curtis, Glen. 2007. "Conducting an Effective Board Evaluation." Directorship 34 (4): 62. http://www. directorship.com/.

De Montesquiou, Aude, Mayada El-Zoghbi, and Alexia Latortue. 2008. "Governments Give Credit," Consultative Group to Assist the Poor. http://www.microfinancegateway.org/p/site/m/template. rc/1.26.9164/.

Giles, Lionel, Trans. 2005. *The Art of War by Sun Tzu: Special Edition.* El Paso, TX: El Paso Norte.

Ledgerwood, Joanna, and Victoria White. 2006. *Transforming Microfinance Institutions.* Washington, DC: World Bank and Microfinance Network.

MicroRate. 2006. "Microfinance Investment Vehicles: An Emerging Asset Class." MFInsights, MicroRate, Washington, DC. http://microrate.com/home/publications/microfinance-research-reports.

OECD (Organisation for Economic Co-operation and Development). 2004. OECD *Principles of Corporate Governance.* Paris: OECD.

Oregon School Boards Association. 2009. "Resources." http://www.osba.org/Resources/LeftNav/Board_Operations.aspx.

Otero, Maria. 2001. "Governance and Ownership of Microfinance Institutions." Microenterprise Best Practices Project Paper, U.S. Agency for International Development, Washington, DC.

Additional Resources

BoardSource. http://www.boardsource.org/.

Branch, Brian, and Christopher Baker. 1998. "Overcoming Governance Problems: What Does it Take?" Paper presented at the Inter-American Development Bank (IDB), Conference on Credit Unions, Washington, DC, March 2.

Bruett, Tillman, ed. 2007. *Measuring Performance of Microfinance Institutions: A Framework for Reporting, Analysis, and Monitoring.* The SEEP Network, Washington, DC.

Brusky, Bonnie. 2004. "Linking MFIs to Commercial Financing in Latin America: Inter-American Development Bank Support of Profund." Case Studies in Donor Good Practices 12, Consultative Group to Assist the Poor, Washington, DC.

Demb, Ada, and F-Friedrich Neubauer. 1992. *The Corporate Board.* New York: Oxford University Press.

Duca, Diane. 1996. *Nonprofit Boards: Roles, Responsibilities, and Performance.* New York: John Wiley & Sons, Inc.

Rock, Rachel, Maria Otero, and Sonia Saltzman. 1998. "Principles and Practices of Microfinance Governance." Microenterprise Best Practices Project Paper, U.S. Agency for International Development, Washington, DC.

Rosenberg, Richard, Timothy Lyman, and Joanna Ledgerwood. 2003. "Regulation and Supervision of Microfinance." Donor Brief 12, Consultative Group to Assist the Poor, Washington, DC.

Annex: Table 2A.1 Sample Board Self-Evaluation Questionnaire

The board of a Kazakhstani microfinance institution used the questionnaire in table 2A.1 to assess its effectiveness.

Please evaluate the following statements according to the scale: 4 – strongly agree, 3 – agree, 2 – disagree, 1 – strongly disagree				
1. Vision and Mission: Is the Board united around a common vision and a shared understanding of strategy for the future? Consider:	**4**	**3**	**2**	**1**
Members of the board have a shared vision of the nature, purpose and priorities of the organization.				
Members of the board demonstrate a common view of the kind of organization it wants to be, as well as of the most important aspects of its performance (i.e. the criteria by which success or failure is to be evaluated).				
The above points are documented.				
This is a board which knows where it is going.				
Your comments:				
2. Roles and Responsibilities: Are the board's responsibilities and the roles of board members clearly defined and understood? Consider:				
The duties of the board, of individual board members, and of board committees, are clearly defined in writing.				
The legal obligations of board members are well understood.				
New board members are adequately briefed about the organization, its history, constitution, activities, aspirations, and performance.				
There is an ongoing process of board training and development.				
Your comments:				
3. Governance Style: Does the Board manage by policy, or by intervention in areas of executive responsibility? Consider:				
The board focuses its attention on "top level" performance indicators and strategic direction.				
The Board looks for feedback on the effective implementation of its decisions without intervening in operational detail.				
The distinct roles of board chair and executive director are documented so that there is no overlap (or gap).				
The Board strives to empower staff to do their jobs subject to periodic performance review without constant board intervention.				
Board committees concentrate on policy and direction and do not slip into "micro-management".				
Your comments:				
4. Board Administration: Is board administration carried out in a fully professional and legally correct manner? Consider:				
Board meetings are correctly and legally administered, including calling notices for meetings, agendas, minutes, annual general meetings, and so forth, as appropriate.				
Board meetings are managed effectively, making good use of everyone's time.				
Board meetings deal with important and strategic issues.				
Processes for the appointment of new board members are documented and are designed so as to ensure a diverse and capable board.				
Your comments:				
Source: Compiled by Tillman Bruett.				

3 INTEREST RATES: PAYING FOR RISK

*Creditors have better memory than debtors.**

Benjamin Franklin

*Benjamin Franklin, 1758, *Poor Richard's Almanac*, http://www.quotationspage.com/quote/29923.html.

Introduction

Access to commercially priced credit can have a positive effect on the welfare of low-income households. Credit can finance new equipment purchases or enable new business opportunities. It can provide better housing or help parents feed, educate, and clothe their children. In addition, it can help households and businesses recover from disaster. However, to provide regular access to credit, microfinance institutions (MFIs) must be able to sustain their operations independently and grow to meet demand.

To that end, MFIs must charge an interest rate that covers their costs and risks and generates a profit. These rates are high compared to banks—sometimes by a large margin. This comparatively high cost of microloans has led to questions about whether MFIs are overcharging and overindebting the poor (see, for example, Epstein and Smith 2007).

This chapter presents data on the rates MFIs are charging their customers and examines the components of microcredit interest rates, especially the pricing of risk. The chapter then addresses the question whether microfinance interest rates are too high and points to a number of key actions MFIs can take to lower rates without jeopardizing institutional sustainability or growth potential. Finally, it discusses the reasons why government policies and programs that aim to lower interest rates by imposing rate ceilings or subsidizing credit usually yield poor results.[1]

Interest Rate Setting

To succeed, MFIs must be able to meet a number of fixed and variable costs and guarantee a certain profit. Costs include operating costs, the cost of funds, and expected loan losses. Operating costs include office space and supplies, employee remuneration and training, transportation and communications, and equipment and building depreciation, among others.

Operational costs often make up the single largest component of the rates MFIs charge borrowers. In a 2002 study, operating (also called administrative) costs were between 10 and 25 percent of the average loan portfolio. In a 2007 study, average operating expenses for 894 MFIs in 94 countries were around 19.2 percent of a loan portfolio (MIX 2007; Rosenberg 2002).[2] Figure 3.1 shows that for a set of sustainable MFIs, average operating costs in 2004 and 2005 accounted for about 10 percent of the interest rates (using returns on loan portfolios as a proxy for interest rates).

---

1. This chapter is based on the June 2007 dialogue with Adrián González (the Microfinance Information Exchange), Juan Buchenau (formerly with the Consultative Group to Assist the Poor, now with the World Bank), and Narda Sotomayor (Superintendency of Banking, Insurance, and Pension Funds, Peru).
2. Rosenberg (2002) includes investment income as a component in his interest rate calculation. This chapter does not discuss investment income, but an MFI should deduct the revenue it earns on its assets, not including its loan portfolio (such as a certificate of deposit), when calculating the interest rate. Where necessary, the MFI might also need to include taxes in its calculation.

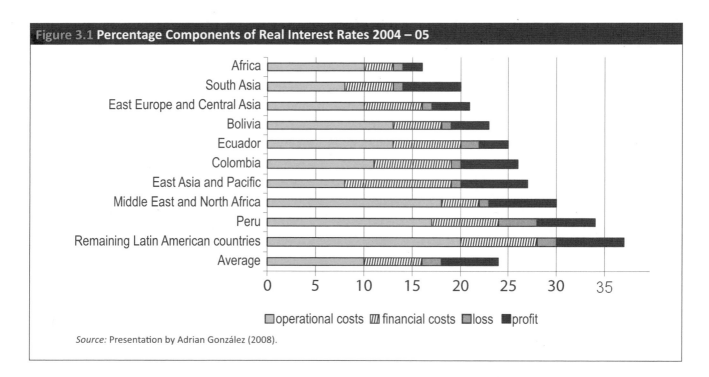

Figure 3.1 **Percentage Components of Real Interest Rates 2004 – 05**

Source: Presentation by Adrian González (2008).

Figure 3.1 also gives an indication of how capital costs contribute to interest rates, as calculated by measuring the MFIs' financial expenses against portfolio returns,[3] which were between 3 and 10 percent. The cost of capital typically includes weighted averages of the rates paid by the MFI on the loans or deposits used to finance its portfolio, as well as the cost of equity.[4] Costs are adjusted for subsidized loans and grants. Self-sustaining institutions paying market rates will have higher financial costs.

Sustainable interest rates also cover the risk that the loan will not be repaid. The risk price can be set on the basis of the historical loan loss rate for the entire portfolio, or it can be estimated and priced for categories of borrowers. The first method is a simple calculation based on the portion of the gross loan portfolio that must be written off due to borrower defaults every year. The MFIs analyzed in figure 3.1 averaged loan losses of about 2 percent of their portfolios, which translates into roughly 2 percentage points in the interest rates that the institutions must charge borrowers, on average.[5]

More complex risk-pricing methodologies assess the probability of default at the client level and assign higher interest rates to riskier classes of borrowers. Using segmented risk-evaluation techniques, for example, one can analyze groups of borrowers with similar characteristics to determine how those characteristics correlate with loan performance. The data and analysis for this segmentation can be drawn from an MFI's own database or, preferably, from a database that contains information from other MFIs, as well as businesses that are likely to have payment and transaction histories for lower-income borrowers (domestic goods retailers, agricultural input suppliers, and mobile phone service providers).[6]

---

3. Financial expenses as defined by Microfinance Information Exchange are the "total of financial expense on liabilities, net inflation adjustment, cost-of-funds adjustment and other expenses from financial services." See González (2008).
4. In theory, the cost of equity is the return shareholders require on the capital they invest in an enterprise. While MFIs rarely have shareholders expecting dividends, Rosenberg (2002) recommends they calculate the expected erosion in the value of their equity caused by inflation and add this component to the cost of capital.
5. A 5 percent loan loss rate would translate into about 5.25 percent as a component of an interest rate calculated using this method, because MFIs must plan to earn enough interest on the loans that are repaid to cover the losses on the larger amount that is lent. See Rosenberg (2002).
6. For more information about the development of credit reporting systems that include data relevant to lower-income borrowers, see the International Finance Corporation's Credit Bureau Knowledge Guide, http://www.ifc.org/ifcext/gfm.nsf/Content/FinancialInfrastructure.

Using data from their own client histories, however, MFIs can improve their assessment of client risk by analyzing how characteristics like gender, length of time at current address, and length of time at current employment correlate with loan performance. From this analysis, the loan officer can determine if a prospective borrower is more or less likely to repay the loan on the basis of the performance of clients with similar profiles. For repeat borrowers, the performance of their past loans also enters in the calculation (Schreiner 2003).

Using segmented risk evaluation along with traditional risk assessment methods, like workplace visits and interviews with references, MFIs can determine which borrowers pose the highest risk of default. Usually, the highest-risk clients are rejected, but other clients may be grouped into risk categories of average to high, average to low, and low, for example. The risk component of the interest rate charged on their loans would then be priced according to the historical loss rates associated with borrowers in their same category.

Finally, the profit component of an interest rate should be determined on the basis of the MFI's growth targets. Without additional equity, the institution is constrained in the amount of money it can borrow and lend to its own clients. To support long-term growth, MFIs should target a capitalization rate between 5 and 15 percent of the average outstanding loan portfolio. Internally generated capital is arguably the best source of new equity because it enables the MFI to expand services to more borrowers or loan more money to existing clients. The MFIs represented in figure 3.1 were earning between 3 and 7 percent returns on their portfolios.

Are Microfinance Interest Rates Too High?

Some observers seem to think that MFIs are taking advantage of their clients with abusively high interest rates. Worldwide, the MFIs for which data are available charge their borrowers an average interest rate of 35 percent (Kneiding and Rosenberg 2008). Is this too much to charge poor people for borrowing money? There are several ways to approach this question. First, from the borrowers' perspectives, the costs and other terms of a loan from an MFI must generally be better than the terms offered by alternative sources. Otherwise, borrowers would not take the loan from an MFI. Indeed, thousands of MFIs extend credit to the poor around the globe. This finding suggests that the price is not a determining factor for a large pool of low-income clients.[7] In addition, while 35 percent may be high compared to rates in mainstream banking, the costs of making many small loans are higher than the costs of making larger loans—box 3.1 explains why. Moreover, most MFIs are not profiting greatly from their customers. Most of those MFIs that report their financial data declare a modest median rate of return on capital of only 1.1 percent.

---

7. See the interview with Richard Rosenberg (CGAP 2008). See also, for example, Rosenberg (2007) and Epstein and Smith (2007). The data suggest that MFI rates are less than informal moneylending charges (CGAP 2008).

Box 3.1 Microcredit Cost Structure

Compare the costs of two hypothetical lenders, Big Lender and MicroLender, each of which lends US$1,000,000. Big Lender makes a single loan, while MicroLender makes 10,000 loans of US$100 each.

The costs of capital and loan loss risk vary proportionally with loan size. Both lenders need to raise US$1,000,000 to fund their loans and will have to pay the same market rate—say, 10 percent—for the money. If both lenders have a history of losing 1 percent of their loans to default each year, they will need a loan loss provision of that amount. Both lenders can cover the cost of their capital and their risk by charging 11 percent (10% + 1% = 11%) on the loans they make to their customers.

Administrative costs are not proportional to loan size. Making a single loan of US$1,000,000 might cost Big Lender US$30,000 (3 percent of the loan amount) in staff time and other expenses involved in appraising, disbursing, monitoring, and collecting the loan. Big Lender can cover all its costs by charging the borrower an interest rate of 14 percent (10% + 1% + 3% = 14%).

However, MicroLender's administrative costs for each US$100 loan will be much higher than 3 percent of the loan amount. Instead of US$3 per borrower, MicroLender is more likely to have to spend US$20 or more per borrower. Big Lender has to deal with only a single borrower, but MicroLender has to deal with 10,000 borrowers who typically do not have collateral, financial statements, or records in the database of a credit reporting bureau. Many of these clients may be illiterate. Lending to and collecting from such clients require time-consuming personal interaction.

If Big Lender's client repays the loan every three months, Big Lender processes only four payment transactions per year. MicroLender's borrowers probably make repayments monthly or even more frequently, generating at least 120,000 transactions per year. While Big Lender's administrative cost is US$30,000 per year, MicroLender's cost is at least US$200,000. Covering this cost requires a 20 percent charge on loaned amounts, resulting in an interest rate of at least 33 percent (10% + 1% + 20% = 33%). Administrative costs may be much higher in young MFIs that are too small to take advantage of economies of scale.

Source: Helms and Reille 2004.

Lowering Interest Rates at the Institutional Level

Yet, many MFIs can achieve substantially lower rates. Operating costs are both the largest and the most manageable component of interest rates, and efficiency gains at the institutional level could significantly lower rates for the industry as a whole. MFIs can use a number of technological innovations (see chapter 8 of this volume) and operational strategies and tactics to improve productivity, better manage risk, and reduce administrative costs.

Operational risk management

Operational risks generally pose the greatest potential threat of loss to an MFI. They include credit risk, and the risk of fraud and theft. MFIs can often greatly reduce the likelihood of losses and contain the scale of their damages by identifying vulnerabilities, designing and implementing controls, and monitoring their effectiveness.[8]

---

8. See the Operational Risk Management course developed by the Consultative Group to Assist the Poor (2009c), http://www.cgap.org/p/site/c/template.rc/1.26.4915/. See also chapter 1 of this volume.

Loan officer incentives

One particularly important way an MFI can reduce the risk of loan losses and generate higher productivity per officer is to create appropriate incentives for loan officers to maintain large and healthy loan portfolios. There are many ways to design an incentive program. For example, the MFI can offer a bonus for each successful loan repayment, or it can target specific productivity measures, like number of clients visited per day.[9]

Management Information Systems

The MFI's management information system is its system of collecting, archiving, retrieving, and using information. The system tracks the loan officers' productivity and clients' repayment schedules and balances, among other things. A good information system is vital for making timely assessments of the quality of the loan portfolio and other variables that most affect cost and risk.[10]

Lowering Interest Rates through Government Policy

Concerned with the high cost of microcredit, governments want to enable microbusinesses and poorer households to have access to cheaper credit to improve productivity and engage in welfare-enhancing economic activities. Governments also want to protect the poor from abusive lending practices. However, two of the most common policy and programmatic tools used by the public sector to achieve these goals—subsidizing credit or setting limits on interest rates—tend to lead to counterproductive results.

Subsidized credit programs are usually administered by state-owned financial institutions or take the form of credit lines extended by the government to public or private lenders at below-market rates. Usually, the subsidized loans are directed toward specific groups of borrowers, like poor women, or specific economic activities, like housing or agriculture.

Such programs often have many repercussions and serious problems. Government institutions may lack the incentives to monitor such loans effectively or control administrative costs, because success is often defined in terms of credit disbursements rather than loan portfolio quality or operational efficiency. Subsidized credit can be an enormous fiscal drain on governments as well, because borrowers often view the loans as lightly disguised grants, with no penalty for incomplete repayment. This perception is especially true in countries with a history of debt forgiveness. Box 3.2 describes other effects of subsidized interest rates.

9. See the MicroBanking Standards Project, http://www.gdrc.org/icm/rating/rate-5.html.
10. See the management information system training offered by the Consultative Group to Assist the Poor (CGAP 2009b).

Box 3.2 Effects of Subsidized Interest Rates

There are a number of important distortions that occur when interest rates are subsidized, for example,

- Subsidized loans distort the opportunity costs of investments, leading to the misallocation of capital to higher-risk and lower-reward opportunities.
- Subsidized onlending rates could result in a lack of financial discipline by the financial institution or its clientele, since cheap loans are often regarded as grants that do not have to be repaid.
- Low-cost loans discourage savings mobilization because the loans preclude remunerative interest rates on deposits.
- Government budget constraints, combined with subsidized interest rates and poor enforcement, mean that fewer borrowers will be served over time.
- Below-market onlending interest rates attract rent seekers and result in credit rationing, which typically favors the wealthy and politically connected.
- Subsidies constrain the financial institution from achieving long-term financial sustainability, since the interest rate is inadequate to cover all operating and financial costs, and thus constrain the supply of credit.
- Withdrawal or cancellation of subsidies by the government or donors could cause financial distress for the financial institution and its client.

Source: Yaron, McDonald, and Piprek 1997.

Governments also try to lower the price of credit by simply mandating that interest rates stay below a preset ceiling. Oftentimes, such policies aim to protect borrowers from abuses. Unfortunately, this approach tends to hurt rather than protect microbusinesses and low-income households by rationing credit artificially. Interest rate ceilings make it difficult or impossible for formal and semiformal microlenders to cover their costs, driving them out of the market (or keeping them from entering in the first place). Potential clients either lack access to finance or must go to informal credit markets, which are generally more expensive (see Helms and Reille 2004). Interest rate ceilings can also lead to less transparency about the costs of credit, because lenders cope with interest rate caps by adding confusing fees to their services. Table 3.1 summarizes the effects on supply and demand for microfinance services when governments impose interest rate ceilings.

Table 3.1 **Effects of Ceilings on Microcredit Interest Rates**

Supply Side	**Demand Side**
Short-term effects	**Short-term effects**
• Lenders are compelled to reduce their rates. • Excess demand creates incentives for rent-seeking among lending staff. • Viability of lending to the poor is reduced. • Lenders' profits on loans to the poor are reduced. • Incentives to make loans to the poor are reduced. • Incentives to increase investments to expand loans to the poor are reduced. • Policy risk on lending to the poor increases (threat of new ceilings). • A negative signal is sent to potential investors. • Risk of lending to microlenders increases. • Incentives to commercial banks to enter the microcredit market are reduced.	• Demand for loans increases at the ceiling rate. • Some new potential clients seek loans at the new rates. • An excess demand for loans is created at the ceiling rate. • Price of credit to some of those who actually get loans is reduced. • Some borrowers pay higher transaction costs than before.
Medium- to long-term effects	**Medium- to long-term effects**
• Microlenders' creditworthiness declines. • Price at which microlenders can borrow in the market increases. • Microlenders' profit declines. • Supply of funds from some donors declines. • Some lenders leave the market. • Supply of loans to the poor declines. • Microlenders' quality of services to the poor declines. • Interest rates paid on deposits are reduced by affected microlenders. • Microlenders increase transaction costs of small deposits. • Supply of microlenders' other financial services to the poor also declines.	• Some borrowers shift to informal commercial markets. • Many former borrowers become worse off because of the decline in supply. • Defaults increase.
Source: Adapted by authors from Fernando (2006).	

Although interest rate ceilings do not have the desired effect, concerns about the high costs of microfinance in many countries are valid, and the government has an important role to play in expanding access to microfinance and lowering its cost. If government can create the market conditions that lead to competition among lenders, evidence exists that lending prices can be driven downward, while access expands. In Peru, for example, rapid growth of the microfinance industry over the past ten years has led to microfinance penetration rates of between 25 and 35 percent of eligible borrowers, and interest rates have been halved over the same period (Mapstone 2009). Policies to promote competition among credit providers encompass a wide range of programmatic and regulatory issues: (1) market intervention, (2) financial sector supervision and regulation, and (3) macroeconomic and trade policies.

Market interventions

Governments can support programs to extend the reach of microfinance. These programs include loan guarantees, grants of technical assistance or equipment to MFIs, or grants to microborrowers to supplement loan funds. Each intervention has its own track record and recognized design and implementation pitfalls.[11]

Financial sector supervision and regulation

In the creation of competition among financial service providers, the regulatory framework is pivotal to providing a level playing field and safeguarding the interests of the households and business. There are many specific issues and topics to consider related to government supervision and regulation as it affects microfinance.[12] Concerns for government's role include decisions about how to (1) apply prudential versus nonprudential regulation (prudential regulations require supervision of the banking authorities), (2) harmonize the treatment of different types of financial intermediaries to avoid regulatory arbitrage, (3) protect borrowers against abusively high rates or aggressive lending practices, (4) promote the development of accessible credit information and payments systems, and (5) enable innovations in the use of technology and institutional partnerships.

Governments can enable significant efficiency gains in microfinance markets by promoting the sharing of credit information, increasing institutional access to the electronic payments systems, and enabling innovations in payments technologies. As important, governments should enforce laws that protect against money laundering and other financial crimes.[13]

Macroeconomic and trade policies

Finally, governments can create an enabling environment for a sustainable and competitive microfinance sector by ensuring a stable macroeconomic environment and allowing the entrance of foreign competitors into the financial markets.[14]

Conclusion

The debate about microcredit interest rates can quickly reach a highly politicized level. Evidence suggests, however, that MFIs are not profiting excessively or charging their borrowers inappropriately high rates. Even at its most efficient, microlending will inevitably cost more than conventional lending. The rates reflect the high costs of delivering small loans to a large number of diverse clients. The alternatives in informal markets represent even greater costs. However, this should not be interpreted as a justification for inefficiency. MFIs have an important role to play in lowering interest rates, and there are many lessons learned they can apply to the task.

While governments may be tempted to force rates downward by imposing interest rate ceilings or subsidizing credit, such means have proven ineffective when it comes to expanding access to affordable credit. Alternatively, governments can help to expand access to financial services and lower the price of microlending through the careful development of a legal and regulatory framework that promotes competition, creates adequate financial infrastructure, enables innovation, and engenders stable financial markets.

---

11. Two good starting points for information are CGAP (2009a) and World Bank (2005).
12. See the U.S. Agency for International Development's microLinks service, http://www.microlinks.org/ev_en.php.
13. See Christen, Lyman, and Rosenberg (2003).
14. See World Bank (2008).

References

CGAP (Consultative Group to Assist the Poor). 2008. "Behind the Headlines: Are Microcredit Interest Rates Exploitative? An Interview with Microfinance Expert Rich Rosenberg," CGAP, Washington, DC, February 15. http://dev.cgap.org/p/site/c/template.rc/1.26.4516/.

————. 2009a. "Government's Role in Microfinance: What Is the Optimal Policy Mix?" http://www2.cgap. org/p/site/c/template.rc/1.26.4903.

————. 2009b. "Information Systems: About the IS Program." http://www.cgap.org/p/site/c/template. rc/1.26.3802.

————. 2009c. "Operational Risk Management Course." http://www.cgap.org/p/site/c/template.rc/1.26.4915/.

Christen, Robert P., Timothy Lyman, and Richard Rosenberg. 2003. *Microfinance Consensus Guidelines: Guiding Principles on Regulation and Supervision of Finance.* Washington, DC: Consultative Group to Assist the Poor.

Epstein, Keith, and Geri Smith. 2007. "The Ugly Side of Microlending." *BusinessWeek*, December 13. http://www.businessweek.com/magazine/content/07_52/b4064038915009.htm.

Fernando, Nimal A. 2006. "Understanding and Dealing with High Interest Rates on Microcredit: A Note to Policy Makers in the Asia and Pacific Region." East Asia Department, Asian Development Bank, Manila.

Franklin, Benjamin. 1758. *Poor Richard's Almanac.* http://www.quotationspage.com/quote/29923.html.

González, Adrian. 2007. "Tasas de interés en instituciones de microfinanzas en América Latina." Paper presented at a workshop at the World Bank, Washington, DC, June.

Helms, Brigit, and Xavier Reille. 2004. "Interest Rates Ceilings and Microfinance: The Story So Far." Occasional Paper 9, Consultative Group to Assist the Poor, Washington, DC.

International Finance Corporation. 2006. "Credit Bureau Knowledge Guide." http://www.ifc.org/ifcext/gfm.nsf/ Content/FinancialInfrastructure.

Kneiding, Christoph, and Richard Rosenberg. 2008. "Variations in Microcredit Interest Rates." Brief, Consultative Group to Assist the Poor, Washington, DC.

Mapstone, Naomi. 2009. "Lending Rivals Bid for Slice of Peru's Market." *Financial Times*, February 27.

MicroBanking Standards Project. http://www.gdrc.org/icm/rating/rate-5.html.

MIX (Microfinance Information Exchange). 2007. "Annual MFI Benchmarks." http://www.themix.org/ publications/2007-annual-mfi-benchmarks.

Rosenberg, Richard. 2002. "Microcredit Interest Rates." Occasional Paper 1, Consultative Group to Assist the Poor, Washington, DC.

————. 2007. "CGAP Reflection on the Compartamos Initial Public Offering: A Case Study on Microfinance Interest Rates and Profits." Focus Note 42, Consultative Group to Assist the Poor, Washington, DC.

Schreiner, Mark. 2003. "Scoring: The Next Breakthrough in Microcredit." Occasional Paper 7, Consultative Group to Assist the Poor, Washington, DC.

U.S. Agency for International Development. http://www.microlinks.org/ev_en.php.

World Bank. 2005. "Meeting Development Challenges: Renewed Approaches to Rural Finance." Approach Paper, Agriculture and Rural Development Department, World Bank, Washington, DC.

————. 2008. *Finance for All: Policies and Pitfalls in Expanding Access*. Washington, DC: World Bank.

Yaron, Jacob, P. Benjamin McDonald Jr., and Gerda L. Piprek. 1997. "Rural Finance: Issues, Design, and Best Practices." Environmentally and Socially Sustainable Development Studies and Monographs Series 14, World Bank, Washington, DC.

Additional Sources

Buchenau, Juan. 2007. "Tasas de interés en microfinanzas y el rol del gobierno." Paper presented at a workshop at the World Bank, Washington, DC, June.

Ghosh, Suman, and Eric Van Tassel. 2007. "Microfinance, Subsidies, and Dynamic Incentives." Working Paper 07001, Department of Economics, College of Business, Florida Atlantic University. Boca Raton, Florida.

González, Adrian. 2008. "Tasas de interés en instituciones de microfinanzas en América Latina." Microfinance Information Exchange, Washington, DC. http://www.themix.org.

Holtmann, Martin. 2001. "Designing Financial Incentives to Increase Loan Officer Productivity: Handle with Care!" *MicroBanking Bulletin* 6 (April): 5–10.

Honohan, Patrick. 2006. *Financial Sector Policy and the Poor: Selected Findings and Issues*. Washington, DC: World Bank.

Hudon, Marek. 2007. "Fair Interest Rates When Lending to the Poor." *Éthique et Économique* 5 (1). http://ethique-economique.net/.

Porteous, David. 2006. "Competition and Microcredit Interest Rates." Occasional Paper 33, Consultative Group to Assist the Poor, Washington, DC.

Sotomayor, Narda L. 2008. *Las tasas de interés en microfinazas: La experiencia de Perú*. Lima: Superintendencia de Banca, Seguros, y Administradora de Fondos de Pensiones.

Wheatley, Jonathan. 2009. "Small is Beautiful for Latin American Financing." *Financial Times*, February 26.

4 MICROINSURANCE: ANTICIPATING CLIENT RISKS

*Microinsurance comes from the heart, but it is a business and not a charity.** Alvaro Uribe, President of Colombia*

*Alvaro Uribe, n.d., http://www.microinsurancecentre.org/UI/Home.aspx.

In microfinance, governments, donors, and microbusinesses share one objective: to build productive assets and smooth consumption so that low-income producers and their families can live better. Donors, governments, and millions of households have invested heavily during the past two decades to create productive assets, and very little has been done to protect them. Unpredictable shocks—hurricanes, earthquakes, and illnesses, among others—affect the most vulnerable businesses and their assets disproportionately. Thus, there is growing interest in developing a menu of risk mitigation products, known collectively as microinsurance. Those products can reduce the economic damage of unanticipated events and can protect low-income households, microbusinesses, and the financial institutions that serve them. This chapter defines microinsurance and discusses the development of microinsurance products and markets, including examples from Latin America.[1]

Insurance Products and Low-Income Clients

Insurance comes in a variety of products; it offers different levels of coverage and is provided by a variety of institutions. The key elements of insurance are payment of a premium, risk pooling, and reimbursement of loss. The insured person, household, group, or business pays a premium in exchange for coverage. Risk pooling enables economies of scale to provide coverage of such events or risks. Insurance reimburses an individual, household, group, or company for some or all of a financial loss that is linked to an unpredictable event or risk.

There are four groups of insurance products: (1) life, (2) disability, (3) health, and (4) property. Table 4.1 lists examples of coverage that each group can provide. Life insurance is one of the most popular; it includes funerals, pensions, endowments, education, and credit (to cover an outstanding loan in the event of the borrower's death. Disability insurance can include partial or total coverage and may offer payments for temporary or permanent disability. Some disability products cover dismemberment, while others include coverage of credit commitments. Health insurance can cover hospitalization, outpatient services, optical and dental services, and specific diseases. Finally, property insurance can cover loss from fire, theft, accident, or natural disaster.

Table 4.1 **Types of Insurance**

Type	Examples
Life	Credit , education, pension, funeral, and endowments
Disability	Permanent and temporary disability; total and partial dismemberment; and debt coverage due to disability
Health	Hospitalization; out-patient, optical, surgical, and dental services; and specific diseases
Property	Fire, theft, agriculture, flood, drought, and prices
Source: Adapted by authors from McCord (2007c).	

Design of the Product for Low-Income Markets

Microinsurance offers an insurance product especially designed for low-income clients—households and microbusinesses. As a match to the cashflow needs of the client, microinsurance products are simple to understand, arrive in a package with other products, and have a low premium. Because most clients have never used insurance, providers typically offer client education as an integral part of the insurance package. The education effort describes the plan's premium, coverage, deductions, claims processing, and payment.

1. This chapter is based on the February 2007 dialogue with Michael McCord (MicroInsurance Centre LLC), Carlos Arce (World Bank), and Héctor Rivas (Financiera FINSOL). Ramanathan Coimbatore also contributed to this chapter.

An effective microinsurance program should be based on an understanding of the priorities and options faced by the poor households in a specific market. The product's promotion, delivery mechanism, and other aspects must be adapted to the special needs and circumstances of poor households and microbusinesses. The product should respond to the client's perceived needs, risks, and ability to pay. These factors are based on local, cultural, and national practices and available services. For instance, in a country with a reliable, free, and accessible public health infrastructure, health insurance needs will be a lower priority. In a community with a strong tradition of mutual support in times of death (such as burial societies), death benefits and coverage will be lower on the list of priorities.[2]

The potential insurance market includes the traditional market (households and businesses wealthy enough to afford insurance) and the microinsurance market (households and businesses just above and just below the poverty line). The very poor and destitute households are best served through state assistance such as government transfers and other programs. Figure 4.1 shows the potential insurance market and the millions who are too poor to afford commercial microinsurance. Table 4.2 compares ex ante risk coverage (with insurance) with ex post results and shows how the costs of shocks can be greatly reduced by insurance.

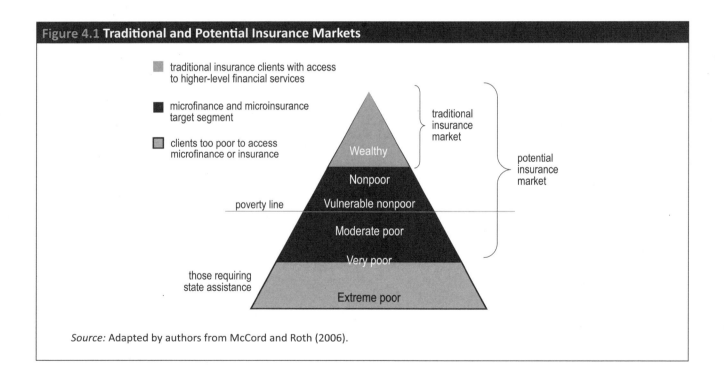

Figure 4.1 Traditional and Potential Insurance Markets

Source: Adapted by authors from McCord and Roth (2006).

Table 4.2 **Risk Coverage and Outcomes**

Ex ante risk protection	Outcomes
Individuals	Crop diversification Intercropping Better land use Income source diversification Asset and inventory accumulation Adoption of new production technologies
Community groups and associations	Risk pooling through group coordination
Ex post risk absorption	**Outcomes**
Individuals and community groups and associations	Migration Asset sales Increased daily labor Human capital decapitalization (withdrawal of children from schools, no health care investment) Mutual community help (in some cases)
Source: Authors.	

If one assumes that low-income households want insurance, how can a microfinance institution (MFI) provide coverage on a cost-effective massive scale? What makes microinsurance attractive to the uninsured and the insurance providers? The MicroInsurance Centre has identified several factors that shape a client's decision to purchase insurance coverage:[3]

- Client's perceptions of insurance
- Client's understanding of how insurance works (premium, coverage, deductibles, and requirements)
- Product matches demand
- Ease of payment
- Cost of coverage
- Client's disposable income
- Cost and frequency of health care or other needs

To be attractive and effective, microinsurance providers need to generate an appreciation of the product through client education. As figure 4.2 shows, often clients set clear priorities. Once a large group of clients has been convinced that microinsurance offers useful protection from high-priority risks, a number of institutions become involved in the definition and delivery of the product. This chain of institutional actors includes the policyholders and beneficiaries, delivery channels, regulated and unregulated insurers, and reinsurance companies (see table 4.3).

---

3. See MicroInsurance Centre LLC (2009).

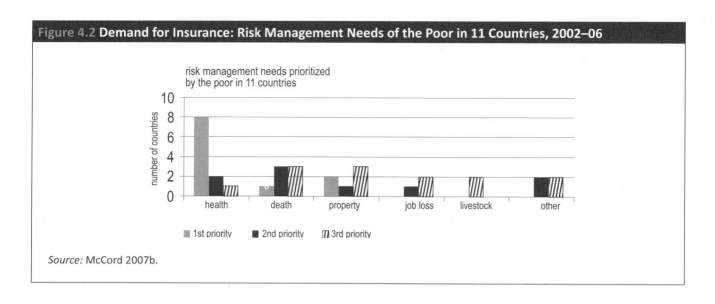

Figure 4.2 **Demand for Insurance: Risk Management Needs of the Poor in 11 Countries, 2002–06**

Source: McCord 2007b.

Table 4.3 **The Microinsurance Supply Chain**

	Who they are	What they do
Reinsurer	Interpolis Re mutual, AXA, Ethiopia index, Swiss Re-India weather index	Cover partial risk of insurer, health and index.
Regulated insurer and unregulated insurer	Multi-national and domestic commercial, mutual, CBOs, NGOs, funeral parlors, informal groups	Manage insurance risk, set pricing, set policyholder requirements, and manage controls.
Delivery channel	MFIs, banks, CBOs, NGOs, agents, employers, government, churches, retailers	Manage contract with policyholders, sell insurance, aid clients with claims, and forward or pay claims.
Policyholder	Individuals, groups	Pay premiums, make claims and buy group coverage for members.
Covered lives	Family members, group members	Have a premium paid.
Beneficiary	Any person or group identified by policyholder	Become identified as a beneficiary on insurance policy, make claim, and receive payment.

Source: MicroInsurance Centre LLC, http://www.microinsurancecentre.org.
Note: CBO = community-based organization; NGO = nongovernmental organization.

Microinsurance for Rural Clients

Beyond traditional livestock insurance, microinsurance providers, governments, and donors have responded to the rural sector's needs with weather-indexed insurance. Because many MFIs have client networks in rural areas, they play an important role in helping rural households, smallholder farmers, and rural microbusinesses improve their risk management practices. This approach includes risks from weather (hurricanes, droughts, floods, El Niño, and La Niña) and other exogenous events.

Weather-indexed insurance, which uses a rainfall index, is the most recent risk management tool available for small agricultural producers. It is effective because the weather outcome (such as the rainfall level) is easily measured in an objective and transparent way. The level can be verified by a specialized institution, and levels are frequently reported (daily if possible). A historical record of the outcome enables the system to set acceptable and unacceptable outcome ranges. In some cases, MFIs provide this product as part of a package of services. The index is based on historical data on rainfall and yields for certain products, and payment is generated automatically after verification.

The most effective indexed insurance systems have transparent contracts, low administrative costs, and standardized contracts for small producers, and they fully cover costs without requiring ongoing subsidies. This approach makes weather the variable, but the specific outcome is chosen because it directly affects the level of crop production and the household income. Examples of these weather variables include rainfall, temperature, and wind. Some indexes use satellites to confirm certain aspects, such as vegetation loss, daily sunshine requirements, animal losses, and hurricane paths to determine affected areas. Box 4.1 provides an example of the mechanism of weather-indexed insurance.

Box 4.1 The Mechanisms of a Weather-Indexed Insurance System

The following illustrates the mechanisms used in a weather-indexed insurance system.

Assume that the expected value of the harvest of a crop is US$10,000. If rainfall is less than 1,000 millimeters (mm) over a specific period, it is considered a drought. The estimated loss of crop sales income has been set at US$10 per mm. Rainfall is measured at 700 mm for the period; the loss is 300 mm of rainfall—resulting in US$3,000 in lost income. This is the amount that would be automatically compensated by the weather-based index insurance system.

Source: Adapted by authors from Arce (2007).

Delivery of the Product

Whether it is a life insurance product, a weather-indexed product, or another type of coverage, the efficiency and scale of coverage depends, in part, on the supply chain. This chain includes all actors involved in the promotion, delivery, servicing, and risk-sharing (reinsurance) required for the effective provision of microinsurance. Table 4.3 illustrates the actors involved and the challenges of coordination that can develop in microinsurance.

The four institutional models to deliver microinsurance are (1) the partner-agent model, (2) the cooperative model, (3) the mutual-based association model, and (4) the community-based model (see table 4.4). Under the partner-agent model, insurance companies underwrite the contracts and agents distribute the insurance products. Under the cooperative model, the insurance company performs both functions of underwriting and distributing the products. Under the mutual-based association model, the owners are the policyholders, but the insurance is professionally managed by an insurance expert. Under the community-based model, local communities are the owners and managers. The organization serves, is accountable to, and is governed by a local constituency with limited resources. Those resources might include the residents of a village or members of a market group, or they might represent single or multiple communities or a network of communities with similar interests.

Table 4.4 **Characteristics of the Four Insurance Delivery Models**

Criteria	Partner-agent	Cooperative	Mutual-based association	Community-based
Ownership	Insurance company	Co-operative (policyholders and owners can be different)	Members of the association (policyholders and owners are same)	Local communities (single or multiple communities or a network of communities)
Objective	Profit-making	Meeting of member needs (profitability is not a motive)	Balance between profit motive and member needs	Service of social needs (profitability is never a motive)
Nature of management	Professional managers who report to the board	Manager with insurance skills (member or external resource)	Professional management by an insurance expert (not a member)	Management by local communities who lack insurance expertise
Distribution mechanism	MFIs, telecom company, utility company, retail stores, post offices, religious institutions	Member offices at the district and municipal levels and through MFIs in case of nonmembers	Distribution at the time of signing up as a member	Network of members who join to receive benefits
Licensing	Licensed under the Insurance Act	Not licensed under the Insurance Act	Licensed to operate insurance	Not licensed
Examples	ICICI Bank and Vimo SEWA (India)	La Equidad (Colombia)	CARD MBA (Philippines)	UMSGF (Guinea)

Source: Goldberg and Ramanathan 2007.
Note: CARD MBA = Center for Agriculture and Rural Development Mutual Benefit Association; MFI = microfinance institution; SEWA = Self-Employed Women Association; UMSGF = Forestry Guinean Mutual Health Organization Union.

Given the distribution networks required to reach large numbers of clients, the most efficient and effective way to achieve large-scale microinsurance coverage is the partner-agent model. This model pairs commercial insurance companies with MFIs, public utility companies, or telecom companies. The insurance company provides the coverage, and the partners provide local knowledge, local networks, and services that can lower costs.

Microinsurance providers can reach large-scale coverage when a reinsurance partner and a clear and supportive legal and regulatory framework are present. Providers are limited in their capacity to underwrite individually each contract without support from reinsurance companies. Reinsurance companies play a huge role in the development of complex microinsurance products and in dissemination of the best practices in the sector.

Simple microinsurance products that cover death, disability, and illness are easy to underwrite because the clients have different risk profiles and their claims do not occur at the same time. More complex products, like index-based weather and livestock insurance policies, represent exposure to events that are difficult to predict and that affect all policyholders at the same time—a drought or excess rain, for example.

Special legal and regulatory issues exist for weather-based insurance products. Regulators should ask whether the product is insurance or a derivative. They will also have operational questions such as the definition of an insurable interest (ownership), the legality of a climate-based index, and the acceptable proof of loss. Regulators may also be concerned with the effect of those products on the soundness of the insurance industry and on the financial sector in general. Such concerns lead to norms on reserve levels and capital adequacy. Finally, regulators should be concerned with consumer protection and transparency, which can be especially challenging when dealing with dispersed rural populations (Arce 2007).

Important reinsurance issues exist with weather-based insurance. Such products can cover the needs and risks of several countries in a region. The World Bank, the International Finance Corporation, the European Development Bank, and Partner Re (a leading international reinsurance company) have contributed €100 million in initial capital to a regional weather-based approach. Services include reinsurance, technical assistance, and data cleaning. This effort became effective in September 2007 and will serve as a model for future programs (Arce 2007).

Clients and beneficiaries should be informed of the coverage, means for registering claims and presenting proof, deductibles, and limitations. They also need to know about changes in policy coverage and requirements. The institutions that have direct and regular contact with the policyholders—MFIs, banks, community-based organizations, the government, churches, or post offices—are the best prepared to guarantee clients and beneficiaries access to this information. The government can also play a role through consumer protection laws and complaint processes that protect clients when purchasing insurance and ensure that their rights are protected in practice.

How Does Latin America Fare in Microinsurance Coverage?

Microinsurance varies widely throughout Latin America and the Caribbean, as a landscape study by the MicroInsurance Centre showed. Map 4.1 shows microinsurance coverage rates in Latin America. The survey on which this map is based focused on the world's 100 poorest countries. The Latin American leaders in this group are Colombia, Peru, and Ecuador, all with relatively good insurance networks. Brazil, Mexico, and other wealthier countries in the region were not included in the survey. Although Brazil and Mexico have low insurance coverage rates for the poor, given their relative size and wealth, the case studies in boxes 4.2 and 4.3 prove that microinsurance is progressing in those countries as well (Roth, McCord, and Liber 2007).

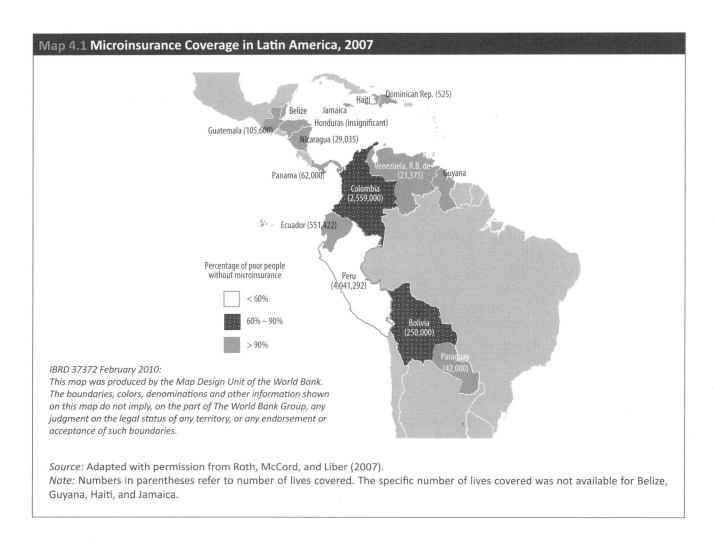

Map 4.1 Microinsurance Coverage in Latin America, 2007

IBRD 37372 February 2010:
This map was produced by the Map Design Unit of the World Bank. The boundaries, colors, denominations and other information shown on this map do not imply, on the part of The World Bank Group, any judgment on the legal status of any territory, or any endorsement or acceptance of such boundaries.

Source: Adapted with permission from Roth, McCord, and Liber (2007).
Note: Numbers in parentheses refer to number of lives covered. The specific number of lives covered was not available for Belize, Guyana, Haiti, and Jamaica.

MFIs and the Barriers to Mainstreaming Microinsurance

MFIs can play a decisive role in the design, delivery, monitoring, and evaluation of microinsurance products and, ultimately, the scale of coverage of such products. They cannot provide the complete package by themselves, but they make very valuable partners for insurance companies, government agencies, and other actors in the microinsurance chain. To maximize the benefits to MFIs of providing microinsurance products, the MicroInsurance Centre recommends the following approach:

- Leverage the market for desired products and terms: Encourage insurers to offer products that respond better to the needs and demands of clients.
- Encourage competition: Use a number of insurers, tender offers, and provide annual policy reviews.
- Improve integration of microinsurance with MFI incentives and policies: Generate appreciation, provide sales incentives, and ensure client education.
- Recognize the value of a broad range of insurance products to MFI clients and indirectly to the MFI itself: Understand the full range of benefits to client and institution to provide additional incentives to push insurers to offer good products and to sell these products in a professional manner to clients.
- Understand your cost structures.[4]

---

4. See MicroInsurance Centre LLC (2009).

Because the delivery supply chain requires close coordination of a number of actors, limitations often exist at various points. The delivery channel must reach large numbers of interested clients, provide appropriate incentives, and respond to claims. Beneficiaries need to develop an appreciation of the benefits of insurance, a product that has odd characteristics compared to loans, grants, and other services. Given the unique needs and sheer number of this pool of uninsured households and microbusinesses, the products should be simple to understand and determined by available delivery channels. As boxes 4.2 and 4.3 illustrate, those principles, along with strong leadership, can have impressive results.

Box 4.2 Mapfre Seguros: Microinsurance in Brazil

In 2003, when Antonio Cássio dos Santos became the chief executive officer of Mapfre Seguros, his first objective was to offer insurance to people in all income segments in Brazil by expanding the network of delivery channels and increasing the product menu. The results have been outstanding. In a span of five years, Mapfre Seguros has covered 3.5 million people through group life and funeral insurance policies, insured 50,000 rural houses, and provided unemployment insurance coverage to 3.7 million people.

Mapfre Seguros achieved massive outreach as a result of three factors: (1) product prices are appropriately based on special mortality tables; (2) product design is based on the risk priorities of the target segment (demand driven); and (3) new delivery channels (retail stores, utility companies, consumer goods companies, and faith-based institutions) were developed. Its emphasis on using different distribution channels to sell demand-driven products at a reasonable price paid huge dividends in terms of outreach and sustainability.

Source: Authors' interview with Antonio Cássio dos Santos, Rio de Janerio, Brazil, March, 2008.

Box 4.3 FINSOL: Life and Funeral Insurance in Mexico

In 2002, a group of financial sector investors created Financiera FINSOL, a regulated, limited objective financial company in Mexico. FINSOL began operations in August 2003, and by mid-2007, it was serving more than 200,000 clients through 105 branches in 28 states. Microcredit methodologies include village banks, solidarity groups, and individual credit. FINSOL also serviced remittances. The next step is the formation of a Popular Financial Society to enable FINSOL to provide a broader range of financial services, including savings.

As the institution evolved, FINSOL's management noticed another gap in the market—a lack of insurance coverage for borrowers. The high costs of promotion and operations and the potential clients' geographic isolation made them unattractive to traditional providers. The MFIs did not have the specific insurance design and delivery skills. Yet, in combination, they could assemble a product that would be attractive to FINSOL clients and marginally profitable for the institutions. Within one year of start-up, FINSOL life insurance had reached more than 180,000 borrowers. The insurance policy includes (1) no required medical examination for coverage, (2) low policy costs, (3) US$3,000 coverage, (4) immediate payout of 30 percent for funeral expenses, (5) remaining payout within three days, (6) coverage of people age 16 to 65, (7) use of a collective policy format, and (8) double coverage for accidental death.

Source: Adapted by authors from Rivas (2007).

Conclusion

The microinsurance industry is still in its infancy, but it can play an important role in the risk management and consumption smoothing of low-income households. It can also contribute to the growth of microbusinesses and their financial service providers. Low-income households and microbusinesses face a wide range of unpredictable shocks, both large and small. These can include slow onset problems (such as a drought) or sudden, devastating shocks (such as hurricanes, earthquakes, and illnesses). Rural producers are also exposed to a series of production-related risks that can be addressed in an efficient and cost-effective way by innovative microinsurance products.

Because of the needs and limitations of clients, microinsurance has important differences compared to commercial insurance. It has special characteristics in design, delivery, claims processing, and premium structuring that make microinsurance an important alternative risk pooling mechanism for the poor. Although alternative models have shown success in some cases, in many countries the path to large-scale microinsurance coverage will be through traditional insurance companies. These companies already have the skills, information, and risk management systems required for microinsurance.

Governments and donors can help to foster the partnerships that can result in large-scale coverage by supporting research to develop actuarial tables, client education campaigns, financial literacy efforts (including insurance), and conferences and exchanges to share experiences in the region.

References

Arce, Carlos. 2007. "Administración de Riesgos para Productores Agropecuarios: Instrumentos Innovadores." Paper presented at a workshop at the World Bank, Washington, DC, February.

Goldberg, Michael, and Coimbatore S. Ramanathan. 2007. "Microinsurance: International Best Practices." Draft paper, World Bank, Washington, DC.

McCord, Michael. 2007a. "Microinsurance Products and Delivery Channels." Paper presented at Access to Insurance for the Poor Workshop, Rio de Janeiro.

———. 2007b. "Microseguros: Una vision general." Paper presented at a workshop at the World Bank, Washington, DC, February.

———. 2007c. "Overview of Microinsurance." Paper presented at a workshop at the World Bank, Washington, DC, February.

McCord, Michael, and Jim Roth. 2006. "What Is Microinsurance?" Microinsurance Focus Notes 1, U.S. Agency for International Development, Washington, DC.

MicroInsurance Centre LLC. 2009. http://www.microinsurancecentre.org/UI/Home.aspx.

Rivas, Hector F. 2007. "Seguro de Vida—FINSOL." Paper presented at a workshop for the World Bank, Mexico City, Mexico, February.

Roth, Jim, Michael McCord, and Dominic Liber. 2007. *The Landscape of Microinsurance in the World's 100 Poorest Countries.* Washington, DC: MicroInsurance Centre LLC.

Uribe, Alvaro. n.d. http://www.microinsurancecentre.org/UI/Home.aspx.

Additional Sources

Consultative Group to Assist the Poor. 2004–06. "The Good and Bad Microinsurance Practice Case Studies." Working Group on Microinsurance, Consultative Group to Assist the Poor, Washington DC. http://www.microinsurancenetwork.org/networkpublication41.php.

———. "Resource Centers." http://www.microfinancegateway.org/p/site/m/template.rc/1.11.48248/.

International Association of Insurance Supervisors and Consultative Group to Assist the Poor. 2007. "Issues Paper." Working Group on Microinsurance Issues, Regulation and Supervision of Microinsurance, Consultative Group to Assist the Poor, Washington, DC.

Siegel, Paul B., and Jeffrey Alwag. 2001. "Viewing Microinsurance as a Social Risk Management Instrument." Social Protection Discussion Paper, World Bank, Washington, DC.

5 Progressive Housing Microfinance: Building One Room at a Time

A house is a machine for living in.[*]

Le Corbusier

[*]Le Corbusier. 1927. *Toward an Architecture*. Trans. John Goodman (Los Angeles: Getty Research Institute, 2007).

Housing is a basic need. It provides security; protection from the elements; and, in the case of microentrepreneurs, a place to conduct business. Housing microfinance provides the financial resources for new or additional construction in small, manageable amounts using an incremental lending approach that mirrors the building process of poor households. In so doing, it can help the poor guarantee themselves a place to live and work. This chapter describes housing microfinance and its progressive housing approach and discusses issues in the design of a housing microfinance product.[1]

The Housing Microfinance Approach

Compared to traditional housing finance, housing microfinance has more flexible requirements. For example, its proof-of-title requirements are less stringent, and it does not require the borrower to finish building the house within a given period. Given this flexibility, microfinance institutions (MFIs) can address the need for decent housing and enhance their portfolios with a housing microfinance program. They can finance land acquisition, new home construction, purchase of a complete house, home improvement, construction of additional rooms or other structures (new bedrooms, a garage, or a workshop), home repair and maintenance, and new or upgraded infrastructure. Moreover, these gradual improvements can contribute to the broader goal of community development and slum improvement (Painter, Campa Sole, and Moser 2006).

In Latin America, the demand for housing finance for the poor remains largely unmet because traditional banks and mortgage institutions will not change their lending practices to meet the needs of the poor. Traditional mortgages and home improvement loans finance the cost of home building in a single loan, usually distributed over the building period. Those loans have strict underwriting requirements that include full legal title to the property and the ability to make monthly payments for a long time. They also require the borrower to complete the building process in a specified time.

The poor usually cannot comply with those requirements. They may be unable to prove title to their property. Or they may be unable or unwilling to commit to a large loan amount or a long repayment period. With a housing microfinance program, MFIs can use the methodologies of microfinance to fill this gap and address the housing needs of the poor based on their own building practices.

Housing microfinance shares a number of similarities with traditional business microfinance, including (1) small loan amounts (compared to traditional housing finance), (2) no collateral requirement, (3) commercial interest rates, and (4) creditworthiness determined by cashflow and character. Its differences from microfinance are in its effect, loan size, nature of the client, and repayment plan. Table 5.1 describes some of the differences between housing microfinance and traditional business microfinance.

---

1. This chapter is based on the January 2008 dialogue with Richard Shumann (Cooperative Housing Foundation, CHF International) and Jesús Ferreyra (MiBanco, Peru).

Table 5.1 **Differences between Microfinance Loan Types**

Traditional microfinance loan	Housing microfinance loan
Effect on borrower's income	Effect on borrower's assets base and possibly income
Small loan amounts (US$100–US$400)	Larger loan amounts (US$250–US$5,000)
Individual or group loans	Individual loans
Repayment capacity based on generation of future income	Repayment capacity based on borrower's current income
Loan maturity of 3–9 months	Loan maturity of 18 months to 4 years
Source: Daphnis 2006.	

The progressive housing approach meets the needs of the poor because they can avoid taking out large loans for long periods, and they can avoid other traditional bank requirements. Compared to traditional housing loans, housing microfinance loans are small (US$250–US$5,000) and are amortized over relatively short terms (between 1 and 10 years). The small amount of the loan makes the debt affordable. Its flexible requirements regarding proof of land title or income also makes qualification easier.

This approach challenges the traditional belief that housing financing requires relatively large loan amounts over long terms with government subsidies to keep the payments affordable. Although progressive housing microfinance programs may face important challenges, they offer considerable benefits for the poor and the MFIs interested in diversifying their product portfolios.

Key elements of the progressive housing loan include guarantees and collateral, technical assistance, cost considerations, institutional arrangements, and subsidies. The role of government is also a critical consideration in designing a housing microfinance product. These issues are discussed in greater detail below.

Guarantees and collateral

Traditional microfinance does not require formal collateral or guarantees. It guarantees payment with devices such as group lending, forced saving, and alternative forms of collateral. Many of these devices, however, may not be appropriate for the relatively higher amounts and longer terms of a housing loan. In housing microfinance, collateral represents an important constraint. The lack of a formal land title means that the client has no formal collateral to offer. Given this lack of land titles and house deeds, MFIs need to be more flexible and to allow clients to use other documents that prove ownership or at least demonstrate a minimum period of residence. Those documents might include tax receipts or public utilities service receipts. Housing microfinance also accepts more flexible forms of guarantee, such as a co-signer (usually with proof of formal sector employment), chattel mortgages, and obligatory savings. The principle is to hold something of value to the borrower to ensure on-time and complete repayment of the loan.

Technical assistance

Housing microfinance products typically include technical assistance in the loan agreement. Some MFIs view technical assistance as an integral part of their progressive housing methodology. Others view this as an additional cost, with little effect on loan repayment. Technical assistance includes help in the design for improving the quality of the building, meeting pre-loan inspections, lowering the costs for appropriate construction materials, and complying with postloan inspections. The MFI may require that borrowers acquire plans, estimates, and other construction services from a list of recommended service providers. To provide the best technical assistance, MFIs should rely on staff construction specialists in addition to loan officers. In either case, the best technical assistance can improve the relationship with the client and the quality of housing construction.

Housing microfinance programs will use a variety of means to secure the staff and human resources for technical assistance, including the following:

- Train loan officers in basic construction budgeting and design.
- Train construction specialists as loan officers.
- Maintain construction specialists in addition to loan officers.
- Require that households acquire plans, estimates, and other construction services from a list of recommended third parties.

Costs and affordability

Interest rates for business microloans are usually higher than for traditional loans because the associated costs of small short-term loans are higher. Because housing credits are larger and have longer repayment terms than do business microloans, origination costs are lower. However, other types of risks can emerge, such as term mismatch and variable interest rates. If the housing loan is not linked to increased production by the microbusiness, the risk of nonpayment increases. To address these and other risks, MFIs must find different long-term funding sources. Most MFIs in developing countries, however, rely on short-term funds from deposits. As a result, housing microfinance is more expensive than traditional microcredit.

Institutional Changes

To be able to offer housing microfinance loans, MFIs will need to adapt themselves to the new product. They will need to complete an internal process of building and strengthening capacities before launching the new product. Most microfinance programs are based on solidarity groups. Housing microfinance provides more individual lending. The loan officers, therefore, will become multiproduct specialists, with some technical knowledge required. The mission of the MFI might change because it will no longer provide only business-related loans.

The MFI's lending methodology can also be affected by a decision to add a housing microfinance product. For example, solidarity groups are not normally used because housing loans tend to have larger loan amounts and longer repayment periods. The MFI would need to assess the entire group's ability to repay the loan. In Latin America, two exceptions to this rule are the infrastructure credits provided by Génesis Empresarial in Guatemala and the land purchase and titling of the Cooperativa Jesús Nazareno in Bolivia.[2]

Subsidies

Subsidies can provide support for microfinance products. However, for MFIs to reach most households, subsidies are not necessary. Microfinance providers prefer subsidies that provide a small interest-rate rebate

---

2. See Génesis Empresarial, http://www.genesisempresarial.com/, and Cooperativa Jesús Nazareno, http://www.jesus-nazareno.coop/.

tied to on-time repayment. For example, a World Bank–sponsored land fund project in Honduras rewarded borrowers who had a perfect on-time repayment record with savings held in accounts established at the start of the loan cycle. Subsidies could also be linked to technical assistance, to lengthen the grace period (lowering the effective interest rate).

Subsidies can serve other important purposes for MFIs and their clients. For example, MFIs might want to use the subsidies to cover land and title formalization processes. Subsidies can also pay for investment in new technologies, thereby lowering loan delivery costs over time (Painter, Campa Sole, and Moser 2006: 18; Robinson 2002).

The Role of Government and Risk Management

Most governments in Latin America have adequate policies for housing microfinance products. However, to mobilize sufficient capital to meet the growing demand for housing microfinance, MFIs and government regulators must meet the challenge of reducing risks, especially after a natural disaster. By reducing the risk of lending to the poor, governments encourage private sector lenders to enter the market. To that end, government regulation should be neither premature nor heavy handed. Governments should avoid interventions that distort the market. Governments can also encourage private sector lenders to enter the market through special programs in underwriting, marketing, servicing, and collateral guarantees.

Examples from Latin America

Experiences in Mexico and Peru demonstrate that housing microfinance can be a profitable business. As those examples show, the average loan size is larger, the loan term is longer, and yet, the outstanding loan portfolio is often smaller than microcredit for working capital. Creative alliances with services providers (such as building materials providers, universities with architecture and engineering students, and supermarkets) can make housing microfinance more affordable and can streamline repayment.

Housing and Habitat Foundation in Mexico (FUNHAVI)

As microfinance has grown and become more sophisticated, housing microfinance has expanded. As of 2007, for example, the housing portfolio of the housing pioneer Cooperative Housing Foundation (CHF International) included US$16.2 million out of a total portfolio of US$79.4 million in 11 countries. CHF International provides housing loans and technical assistance. Its credits range between less than US$1,000 to more than US$3,000. The repayment periods are between 12 and 18 months.[3]

One of CHF International's most successful programs is the Housing and Habitat Foundation (Fundación Habitat y Vivienda A.C., FUNHAVI). Established in 1996, FUNHAVI began as a pilot program to support community banks and provide health services to the newly arrived workers in the assembly plants (maquilas) in Ciudad Juárez, Mexico. Two years later, recognizing a growing need for housing, FUNHAVI implemented a full-scale housing microfinance program. Loans range from US$510 to US$2,590, with an average loan size of US$1,550. During its first 10 years, FUNHAVI made loans worth a total of US$8.2 million to more than 5,300 low-income families. FUNHAVI now operates in three locations in Ciudad Juárez and one in

---

3. See CHF International, http://www.chfinternational.org.

the city of Chihuahua, and plans to open three more locations in the following year. It is noteworthy that the progressive housing loans are small (average loan balance of US$716), but the short-term portfolio quality risks are significant (with portfolio at risk over 30 days over 30 percent). Table 5.2 shows standard performance indicators as of December 31, 2007.

Table 5.2 **FUNHAVI Performance Indicators, December 31, 2007**

Number of active loans	1,138
Value of loans	US$866,516
Average loan balance	US$716
Loan portfolio as percentage of total assets	75.6
Women as percentage of total borrowers	40
Portfolio at risk over 30 days (percent)	30.2
Source: CHF International, http://www.chfinternational.org/.	

FUNHAVI's success is based on a simple, streamlined three-step process that includes technical assistance, the innovative use of partners, and the necessary safeguards to minimize credit diversion and misuse of funds. The loan preparation process lasts no more than 15 days. Households must demonstrate a monthly income of twice the minimum wage. No savings or credit history is required, but the client must be able to show recent pay stubs, provide the name of a guarantor, and offer proof of land (a less stringent requirement than formal land title). In addition, the community where the house is located must be stable. It cannot be in a flood plain, close to a river, or subject to intensive erosion.

Technical assistance consists of a 30-minute educational presentation to ensure that clients understand their rights and responsibilities and basic information about suppliers and budgets and a visit by an architect who reviews the construction plans and provides a budget for materials and labor. The architect's service fee of US$22 is the only charge in the loan preparation process. Most households take advantage of the architect's service. Very few clients leave the program after this stage (Daphnis et al. 2002; Goldberg and Motta 2003; Schumann 2008).

SOFOLs in Mexico

Another successful example of the growth of the housing microfinance market in Mexico is the Limited Objective Financial Society (Sociedad Financiera de Objeto Limitado, SOFOL). The SOFOLs emerged out of the reorganization of the financial sector that resulted from the North American Free Trade Agreement. In the past decade, they have grown to cover a significant part of the housing microfinance market.

SOFOLs are specialized financial institutions that grant mortgages and consumer, automotive, agricultural, and working capital loans, among others. They serve the middle- and lower-income market. When mortgage SOFOLs began operations, there were no sources of funds. In December 1994, the "Tequila Crisis" resulted in the biggest economic crisis in Mexican history and the collapse of the Mexican banking system. Because the SOFOLs were just starting operations, they had no loan portfolio and were not affected by the crisis. As a result, the mortgage SOFOLs soon became the sole intermediaries of government-sponsored mortgage products.

In 2006, 58 SOFOLs managed US$20 billion—2.6 percent of gross domestic product. With 10 percent of the credit market, they competed successfully with commercial banks that had returned to the market. Mortgage loans represented 63 percent of this portfolio. Less than half of the funds come from development banks; public markets provide 30 percent (Campos Spoor 2006).

MiCasa in Peru

The success of the two Mexican MFIs is mirrored in Peru's MiBanco, the country's first for-profit, fully regulated commercial microfinance bank (and a member of the ACCIÓN International Network). MiBanco offers an extensive menu of microfinance products. MiCasa, the largest of MiBanco's five progressive housing products, finances up to 100 percent of the costs to complete a house. These housing projects may also involve expanding or adding a microbusiness workshop. Maturities range from a minimum of three months to a maximum of five years. The minimum amount of the loan depends on the credit evaluation. With a few exceptions, the maximum loan amount is US$10,000. As of the end of 2007, MiCasa's portfolio exceeded US$50 million (see table 5.3).

Table 5.3 **MiCasa Portfolio, December 2007**

Loan Amt (US$)	Total loans (US$ millions)	Percentage of portfolio	Number of credits	Percentage of number of credits
< 1,000	3.20	6.5	6,703	27.2
1,001–1,660	5.50	11.0	5,347	21.7
1,661–3,330	12.70	25.3	6,596	26.8
3,331– 6,660	15.80	31.3	4,230	17.2
6,661–10,000	12.60	25.0	1,731	7.0
> 10,000	0.45	0.9	37	0.2
Total	50.25	100.0	26,644	100.0
Source: Ferreyra 2008.				

Lessons Learned

Lessons learned by MiCasa and the other MiBanco progressive housing products include the importance of providing a demand-driven product with efficient service and ongoing follow-up. Moreover, the products' sales staffs have learned not to push a particular product: it is more effective for clients to choose from a menu of housing loans. Finally, it is important to set realistic and progressive goals and include results-based follow-up plans to ensure timely completion of the work and on-time loan repayment.[4]

According to a survey of managers in Latin America (Mesarina and Stickney 2007), the benefits of a housing microfinance program include the following:

- Added stability to the overall portfolio, given the seasonal fluctuations in business lending
- Diversification of risk for a portfolio dedicated primarily to working capital loans
- Increased revenue from existing (business loan) clients without incurring significant additional operating costs
- High portfolio quality, which, in turn, implies lower costs in pursuing delinquent loans

---

4. See MiBanco, http://www.mibanco.com.pe.

- Lower administrative costs per amount lent, as a result of longer loan terms
- Increased loyalty and relationships between the customer and the MFI because customers and their families hold strong emotional attachments to their homes

Designing a New Housing Microfinance Program

The experiences of these MFIs and others have led to a number of general insights in the design and delivery of a housing microfinance product. An MFI wishing to design a new housing microfinance product should begin by assessing whether the new product is consistent with its mission and whether the product will further its goals and objectives (see also box 5.1). The MFI should further decide whether the incremental lending methodology is consistent with its own lending methodology and technical assistance facility and how this new product will affect current clientele. This assessment should further include an evaluation of the competition (or potential collaborators) and the legal and regulatory context. The MFI should have a well-established liquidity management system in place.

Box 5.1 Can Gender be a Factor in a Housing Microfinance Program?

In housing microfinance, it is difficult to establish a separate loan category based on gender—unlike other solidarity or communal banking programs. For the most part, a loan is made to the person who holds the title to the house or land. Gender is not relevant. The loan is based on the household's current income. However, in most MFIs, women tend to benefit more than men because they represent a lower credit risk.

Source: Authors.

Given the maturity of housing microfinance products, the MFI will need access to long-term funding. This access will avoid maturity mismatch between its liabilities and its housing loan portfolio. Finally, the MFI should assess whether the new product will increase operational expenses, require new staff members, or lead to important systems changes.

The MFI could also establish strategic business partnerships with suppliers of building materials, as in the case of MiBanco in Peru and FUNHAVI in Mexico. Those partnerships should lead to lower costs for the borrower. In MiBanco's case, this arrangement might evolve into financing partnerships and enhance the lender's ability to reach more potential borrowers. With FUNHAVI, the partnership has led to low-cost integrated technical assistance on design, building materials selection, and construction inspection.

Step 1: Assess the market[5]

Recent experience provides some lessons learned in the design and management of a housing microfinance loan program. For example, the design of the product should begin with a market assessment. This assessment should develop a household survey and include the following:[6]

---

5. This section is adapted by authors from Ferguson (2004).
6. Ferguson 2004.

- Basic information on household income and expenses
- Business income and cost information for microbusiness operators
- Conditions and amount of existing informal and formal debt
- Potential demand for microloans by loan size and type, collateral, interest, and term
- Savings
- Bank and nonbank financial services used by the household
- Condition of home: number of people in house, type of home, roof type, kitchen, bathroom, bedrooms, other rooms, and improvements performed over past five years
- Need and potential for home improvement and other real estate investment

The market analysis will result in estimates of the potential effective demand for various products and, combined with other data, the client's capacity to repay. In general, housing microfinance lenders use affordability ratios similar to those of traditional mortgage finance. The MFI should also assess the types of housing improvements the potential clientele are contemplating. It is also important to understand how such clientele have financed home improvements in the past. In addition, the MFI should assess whether the target clients are willing to borrow the funds and under what conditions (such as interest rate, maturity, grace period, and lump sum or installment payments).

Step 2: Assess the MFI

Further, the assessment should include a review of the MFI, its mission, and its capacities. Given that a housing program is different from other credit programs, the MFI should assess whether such a program is consistent with its mission and goals, and whether it has the capacity (financial and human) to launch and maintain a new product. The MFI should consider whether redirecting financial and human capital from other areas to housing is the best use of resources, given the need for technical assistance and the other differences described previously.

Step 3: Develop a loan product

After completing a market assessment and making the commitment to a housing loan program, the MFI should begin designing the appropriate loan product. The goal of this process should be to develop an affordable and responsive loan product while ensuring the MFI's long-term financial viability. This design includes the interest rates, loan repayment period, technical assistance, and an assessment of the real effective return.

The repayment period largely drives credit risk—usually more than the payment amount. Best practice calls for repayment terms between 1 and 10 years—with an average of between 2 and 5 years—and small loan amounts. Low- and middle-income households can commit to monthly payments for short periods. In fact, the lowest middle-income families prefer to commit to the shortest repayment period possible.

The effective rate of return for these small amounts and short repayment periods results in relatively high returns for the MFI, as much as 27 percent in Latin America. However, this apparently excessive return is necessary to ensure the MFI's financial viability. The return is very likely to decline as competition grows with more lenders entering the market.

The new product will also affect the MFI's organizational structure, management, capacities, and cost structure, among others. For example, the MFI should decide whether it would be more efficient to train a few specialist staff members to manage housing loans, or to train all staff members as generalists. The MFI will need to review its information technology, accounting, and reporting systems. It will also need to determine the cost of launching the new product and how related costs of training, transport, and marketing will affect the institution's bottom line. Finally, the MFI will need first to consider external factors, such as the competitive environment, the potential for strategic alliances with other institutions, and the inflation and other macroeconomic elements, and second to test the product with a sample of clients.

References

Campos Spoor, Manuel. 2006. "The Expansion and Future of Sofols in Mexico." Paper presented at the Housing Finance Systems in Emerging Economies World Bank Group Conference, Session 3 titled "The Role of the Specialized Housing Lenders," World Bank, Washington, DC, March.

Daphnis, Franck. 2006. "Housing Microfinance: Current Issues, Opportunities, and Challenges." Paper presented at a workshop at the World Bank, Washington, DC, January.

Daphnis, Franck, and Bruce Ferguson, eds. 2004. *So, You Want to Do Housing Microfinance: A Guide to Practice.* Bloomfield, CT: Kumarian Press.

Daphnis, Franck, Kimberly Tilock, Thea Anderson, and Ingrid Fulhauber. 2002. "FUNHAVI's Housing Microfinance Program." Civis: Shelter Finance for the Poor Series 4, November.

Ferguson, Bruce. 2004. "Scaling Up Housing Microfinance: A Guide to Practice," *Housing Finance International* 19 (1): 3–13. International Union for Housing Finance, September. http://findarticles.com/p/articles/mi_qa5441/is_200409/ai_n21358126.

Ferreyra, Jesús. 2008. "Productos para Vivienda—MiCasa." Paper presented at a workshop at the World Bank, Washington, DC, January.

Goldberg, Michael, and Marialisa Motta. 2003. "Microfinance for Housing: The Mexican Case." *Journal of Microfinance* 5 (1): 51–76.

Le Corbusier. 1927. *Toward an Architecture.* Trans. John Goodman (Los Angeles: Getty Research Institute, 2007).

Microfinance Information Exchange Market. 2008. FUNHAVI institutional summary. http://www.themix.org.

Mesarina, Nino, and Christy Stickney. 2007. "Getting to Scale in Housing Microfinance: A Study of ACCIÓN Partners in Latin America." *InSight* 21 (May).

Painter, David, Regina Campa Sole, and Lauren Moser. 2006. "Scaling Up Slum Improvement: Engaging Slum Dwellers and the Private Sector to Finance a Better Future." Paper presented at the World Urban Forum III, Vancouver, Canada, TCG International LLC, June, and World Bank, Washington, DC.

Robinson, Marguerite S. 2002. *The Micro Finance Revolution, Volume 2: Lessons from Indonesia.* Washington, DC: World Bank.

Schumann, Richard. 2008. "Microcrédito para Vivienda: Experiencia de CHF International." Paper presented at a workshop at the World Bank, Washington, DC, January.

Additional Source

Pantoja, Enrique. 2002. "Microfinance and Disaster Risk Management: Experiences and Lessons Learned." Draft final report, World Bank, Washington, DC.

6 MICROLEASING: OVERCOMING EQUIPMENT-FINANCING BARRIERS

The machine does not isolate man from the great problems of nature, but plunges him more deeply into them.

Antoine de Saint-Exupery*

*Antoine de Saint-Exupery, BrainyQuote, http://brainyquote.com/quotes/quotes/a/antoinedes131176.html.

Most business owners would probably agree with Saint-Exupery—although machinery holds the key to increasing production, it comes with a cost. Acquiring new machinery can mark the evolution from artisan production to more specialized and efficient production, but it can also mean plunging the business more deeply into problems in the short term. Growing microbusinesses crave new equipment as a path to growth and greater efficiency, but they must confront the costs of increased financial commitments, worker training, wasted materials during the learning process, installation costs, maintenance obligations, increased energy use, and more security.[1]

On the financial side, the lack of sufficient collateral and audited financial statements may prevent the owner from approaching traditional banks. Leasing offers an alternative to a traditional bank loan. A leasing arrangement guarantees access to new machinery while avoiding the long-term problems of traditional loans. Leasing is a financial product that enables businesses to rent new machinery for a defined period of time without providing collateral or increasing debt. For the microfinance institutions (MFIs), microleasing provides new opportunities for long-term financial relationships with growing microbusinesses.

The Basics of Microleasing

The two types of equipment-leasing arrangements are the financial lease and the operational lease. In a financial lease, the client pays the full price of the equipment, plus interest, in installment payments throughout the lease period. At the end of the lease period, the client may purchase the equipment outright for a nominal amount (usually the remainder of the asset's cost). A financial lease can be cancelled only by mutual agreement. In an operational lease, the client rents the equipment for a specified period, at the end of which the client returns the equipment, buys it outright, or renews the agreement. The client may cancel the agreement and return the equipment before the end of the lease period. Because MFIs more commonly offer financial leases and rarely offer operational leases, this chapter focuses on financial leases, their advantages, taxes, regulations, and management considerations and provides some examples from Latin America. The chapter ends with some recommendations for a microleasing program.

Advantages of Leasing for Microbusinesses

From the microbusiness owner's point of view, the advantages of microleasing are related to collateral, payment flexibility, and a chance to upgrade technology after a specific period of time. In financial terms, collateral is far less of a constraint with a leasing contract than if the microbusiness were to apply for a long-term loan to purchase machinery or equipment. Collateral is built into the lease, because the title of the equipment remains with the lender until the end of the contract.

There are important cashflow advantages for the microbusiness. The leasing arrangement's fixed-rate financing makes the arrangement "inflation friendly." As costs for energy, rent, and labor increase, the client pays the same amount each month throughout the lease period. The upfront cash outlay is typically less. Because the lease usually covers 100 percent of the asset purchase, the client does not need to make a large initial down payment in cash. This arrangement means that the business can use its own funds for its working capital needs. Leasing payments can also be structured to match a business's cashflow—whether through a grace period, balloon payments, step-up or step-down payments, deferred payments, or even

1. This chapter is based on the October 2007 dialogue with Glenn Westley (Inter-American Development Bank) and Eduardo Gutiérrez (National Ecumenical Development Association, Bolivia).

seasonal payments. Leasing does not affect the solvency of the firm, because it is not reflected in the liabilities of the balance sheet.

The client also benefits in operational ways. In many leasing programs, the microbusiness operator can choose the supplier and the equipment without intervention or limitations placed on the choice by the MFI. Leasing also offers easy-to-understand lending terms and does not require a large amount of documentation. Finally, a wide range of equipment can be provided by an MFI through a leasing arrangement, as the experience of the Savings and Agricultural Credit Cooperative Society in Madagascar illustrates (see box 6.1).

Box 6.1   CECAM's Expanded Menu of Leased Equipment for Rural Producers

Begun in 1993 in the highlands of Madagascar, the Savings and Agricultural Credit Cooperative Society (Caisses d'Epargne et de Crédit Agricole Mutuels, or CECAM) provides a menu of financial services to its members, who are rural producers. One product is a credit to acquire assets such as plows, harrows, carts, weeding machines, seeders, grinders, husking machines, dairy cows, draught oxen, and tractors. Other products include tools used by carpenters, blacksmiths, mechanics, masons, tailors, and weavers. The lease price is set on the basis of the initial value of the equipment, plus interest and costs related to the transaction. The ownership of the equipment shifts from CECAM to the member after the final payment is received. Unlike most leasing arrangements, CECAM offers both individual and group-based leases of equipment.

Source: Adapted by authors from Fraslin (2003).

Advantages of Microleasing for the MFI

In microleasing, the MFI maintains the ownership of the asset until the final payment is received. As a result, the MFI can offer financing with a smaller or no initial payment, fewer external guarantees, and longer terms (compared to a long-term loan provided for the same purpose). In general, individual leasing arrangements are preferred, because a lease in the name of a community group or cooperative can lead to difficulties in the event of seizure, according to experiences in other countries. In some countries, equipment leasing is exempted from the interest rate ceilings imposed on lending.

Another key advantage of financial leasing is the MFI's strong legal position for repossession of the asset if the client fails to make the required payment. Because it is the owner, the MFI can repossess the equipment. The client is more likely to allow the MFI staff to come onto the property if this right is established in the lease agreement. For this reason, the National Ecumenical Association for Development (Asociación Ecuménica de Desarrollo, or ANED) and Caja Los Andes (both in Bolivia) prefer leasing to long-term loans to finance new equipment.[2] In addition, a court judgment is not necessary for the recovery of the machinery, because the MFI is free to recover and sell the equipment in a secondary market (for used equipment) in the event of default. Therefore, leasing companies prefer more standardized goods (such as taxis, sewing machines, or tractors), which can easily be resold locally. More specialized equipment presents a problem if seized, because there may be far fewer potential buyers.

---

2. However, if the machinery is installed, this advantage could be largely lost. The increased physical costs may make recovery no longer practical.

The process of repossessing the equipment can vary. In Bolivia and Ecuador, repossessing equipment takes only one or two months (compared to one or two years in the case of a defaulted loan). In Ecuador, the MFI submits a standard packet of documents to a judge and obtains an order to repossess the equipment. The process is unilateral and functions well without the need for a police escort. It is fairly inexpensive, between 1 and 2 percent of the total lease value. In Chile, Colombia, El Salvador, Honduras, and Mexico, the laws and procedures are similar for the recovery of leased equipment.

Tax and Regulatory Considerations with Microleasing

Although leasing may make financial sense, tax considerations may outweigh the benefits. For formally registered microbusinesses, the tax advantages or disadvantages change according to the country. Advantages are greater when accelerated depreciation is permitted for the equipment. In some cases, the tax codes favor equipment leasing. In other cases, they introduce a bias for equipment loans. Under some national tax codes, the client can deduct principal and interest from taxable income. For the MFI's informal business clients, the depreciation expense deduction from taxes disappears, and loans can be more effective than microleasing.

From the MFI's perspective, the tax considerations affecting leases include value added taxes (VATs), equipment stamp taxes, and any special tax and regulatory treatment of financial leases. In some countries, an MFI can reduce its tax burden by deducting the depreciated value of the leased equipment, because it retains formal ownership during the life of the lease. In other countries, taxes are charged on the total lease amount (both principal and interest). In addition, different countries apply the VAT differently. In some cases, the VAT is applied against the lease charge but not to a loan. Examples of other taxes include a stamp tax on equipment with a value over US$27,000 (Colombia), an asset tax (Mexico), and a tax on imported equipment (Romania). Although the MFI (as the asset owner) pays those taxes, it can pass them on to the client as part of the transaction costs included in the lease.

Regulatory issues can play an important role in expanding or limiting microleasing. For example, governments unnecessarily limit the market by requiring a subsidiary specialized in leasing. The lack of clear definitions for leasing and the responsibilities and rights of each party in a leasing contract also limit the market's expansion. However, in some countries, equipment leasing is exempted from the interest rate ceilings imposed on lending. The advantages and disadvantages of leasing, compared to long-term lending, are summarized in table 6.1.

Table 6.1 Advantages and Disadvantages of Financial Leases

Factors	Advantages	Disadvantages
Legal enforcement	The MFI has a strong legal position to repossess and sell equipment if the client does not pay the lease.	There can be a greater potential for misunderstanding and legal disputes.
Costs	Enforcement costs are lower.	Set-up costs are higher. Operational costs are higher.
Regulatory aspects	Often, regulations do not impose interest rate caps for leasing.	Banking regulations sometimes prohibit financial leasing or limit it to a special subsidiary, making it harder for an MFI to start a leasing product.
Tax issues	Possible tax deduction or other advantages are available for formal businesses that pay the VAT and utilities taxes.	No tax advantage occurs from leasing for informal firms.

Source: Adapted by authors from Westley (2007).

Management of Microleasing Risks

The most important risk is the possibility that the client will default on the scheduled lease payments. In that case, the MFI, as the equipment owner, can more easily seize the equipment than under the terms of a defaulted loan. As discussed earlier, repossession, therefore, offers greater security to the MFI in a microleasing arrangement. However, in the event of default by the client, the MFI also faces the risk of paying the costs to remove, store, and secure the repossessed equipment.

Another risk for financial leases is damage to the leased equipment. Damages may result from any number of causes, including poor maintenance, improper use, or inappropriate modifications. For example, improper installation or electrical surges could affect the performance of the equipment. Because the client does not own the asset during the life of the lease, the client has little incentive to maintain the equipment or to avoid damaging it during the life of the lease.

To reduce damage risks and costs, the MFI may charge a damage deposit at the beginning of the lease period, but this is not a perfect solution. The amount may not be sufficient to cover the costs of maintaining the equipment or fixing the damage. Moreover, the client may not be able or willing to pay to fix the equipment at the end of the lease period. Some MFIs address damage risk by making arrangements to maintain the equipment during the lease period and billing the client for the service. They also make regular visits to confirm that the client is using the equipment properly. Some MFIs turn to insurance policies to cover related risks, such as theft and injuries to workers, including life insurance for deaths related to the use of leased equipment. Finally, the MFI may offer to sell the equipment to the client at a low price at the end of the lease period. This option assumes that the lease has covered the initial cost of the equipment, plus interest.

Use of Microleasing in Latin America

Microleasing is a new field of business and is not yet part of mainstream microfinance in Latin America. In 2002, a survey of 25 MFIs in 12 Latin American countries reported that equipment financing (including leasing) represented, on average, 21 percent of business. Most of this financing was in medium- to long-term loans. Only two MFIs reported using leasing to finance equipment purchases in any significant way: ANED in Bolivia (with 6 percent of the portfolio) and Inversiones para el Desarrollo in Chile (with 52 percent).

Other institutions in the survey reported that they had considered equipment leasing programs, but government policies discouraged them from moving forward. For example, in Bolivia, a new law required the creation of a subsidiary for leasing programs. As a result, Banco Procredit Los Andes discontinued its leasing program, and two other MFIs—Fundación para Alternativas al Desarrollo and Pro Mujer—never advanced beyond expressions of interest (Westley 2003).[3] As General Manager for Financiera Arrendadora Centroamericana, S.A. (Finarca), Hugo Paguaga Baca said, "It is always good to have a regulatory framework in place, but it shouldn't be a noose that is going to strangle the industry" (Goldberg 2008). The experiences of ANED (Bolivia), Finarca (Nicaragua), and América Leasing (Peru) show how industry leaders have launched leasing programs to respond to demand for asset purchases.

ANED, Bolivia

Beginning in 1997, the Bolivian MFI, ANED, developed a leasing program in response to client demand for resources adapted to their needs for operational and investment capital.[4] In 2004, the program was redesigned

---

3. See IADB (2009b).
4. See National Ecumenical Development Association, http://www.aned.org/.

with support from the Inter-American Development Bank (IADB).[5] The purpose of ANED's microleasing program is to improve access to medium- and long-term financing, according to the productive and investment needs of the microbusiness sector. Equipment and machinery made available by ANED's microleasing program include farm implements; machinery for carpentry shops, bottling plants, and energy; and equipment for small industry (such as welders and compressors). Drawing on its experiences to date, ANED is expanding the program to meet its clients' demand for livestock.

ANED has assessed the advantages and problems of financial leasing. The advantages include (1) elimination of guarantees, (2) the availability of a long-term financial arrangement, (3) a payment schedule that fits the firm's cashflow, and (4) lower transaction costs. ANED recognizes only two disadvantages to microleasing: those related to taxation and property. There is a 13 percent tax on value added, a 3 percent tax on interest payments, and another 3 percent tax on the purchase at the end of the lease.

ANED's leasing program resolves the problem of inadequate or no guarantees. It incorporates productive technology and supports and strengthens the credit products already available. The leasing program has ultimately led to the establishment of strategic alliances among providers and, ultimately, has improved the supply of machinery and equipment. Finally, it strengthens the relationship between the small producers and the farmers, who were not originally seen as a potential market. ANED's Web site provides information on needed equipment across the country to enable businesses and suppliers to carry out transactions efficiently.

Finarca: Leasing to micro and small businesses in Nicaragua

In 1997, Finarca launched its leasing operations in Nicaragua as the first leasing company licensed by the Superintendency of Banks and Other Financial Institutions.[6] The International Finance Corporation (IFC) helped with technical assistance and investment capital.[7] The company evolved quickly after 2000, when the Superintendency permitted it to offer a range of financial services, including working capital loans, consumer loans, housing finance, and letters of credit. Three years later, Finarca's success in leasing and lending attracted the attention of Corporación Interfin, which initially bought 25 percent of Finarca's shares (later purchasing a total of 51 percent). Later, Scotia Bank of Canada acquired Corporación Interfin and eventually took sole ownership of Finarca as well.

Finarca has grown in two directions: (1) it expanded its range of leases, and (2) it moved into rural parts of Nicaragua to find new clients. With assistance from the IADB, Finarca recently launched a new program to lease equipment (tools, machinery, and other productive assets) to at least 300 microbusinesses and small enterprises. The client firms can have up to 15 workers and US$20,000 in total assets. The maximum financing ranges from US$3,000 to US$8,000, with maturities from 12 months to 48 months and with commercial rates of interest. Eligible projects and products for leasing include industrial machinery, warehouse equipment, vehicles, hotel and restaurant supplies, tractors and agricultural machinery, photocopiers and other office equipment, and computers and communications equipment. As of June 2008, Finarca had a portfolio of US$18.8 million in leases, representing 85 percent of its total assets.

---

5. See IADB (2009a) and National Ecumenical Development Association, http://www.aned.org.
6. See Financiera Arrendadora Centroamericana, S.A., http://www.finarca.com.
7. The IFC has worked with financial institutions with leasing products in a variety of countries in Africa, Central Asia, Eastern Europe, Latin America, and the Middle East.

América Leasing, S.A., and the IFC in Peru

América Leasing, S.A. is a specialized leasing company supervised by the Peruvian Superintendent of Banks and Insurance companies.[8] It began operations in 1995 and currently offers financial leases to microbusinesses and to small and medium-size enterprises.

América Leasing is the largest company in Peru that specializes in leasing and that is not part of a banking group. As of December 2006, the company held a 6.5 percent share of the Peruvian leasing market (measured by portfolio amount) and a 14.1 percent market share (measured by number of contracts). It is primarily involved in the transportation, industrial, and commercial segments of the leasing market, which together represent 60 percent of the company's leasing portfolio.

América Leasing's low average lease amount reflects the size of its target segments—small and medium-size enterprises. As of December 2006, 91 percent of the company's portfolio was in business with less than US$21 million in annual sales. The average size of its contracts was US$67,700, compared to US$149,800 for the overall leasing market. The diversified leasing portfolio reached US$127.5 million, with 1,877 active clients in transportation (26 percent), trade (18 percent), industry (16 percent), and equipment (14 percent).

In support of América Leasing's expansion plans, the IFC provided a US$10 million loan and a technical assistance program in 2007. The project helps the company fund its portfolio growth, diversify its financing sources, and strengthen its presence in the small and medium-size enterprise segment.

Recommendations for a New Microleasing Program

MFIs planning to offer long-term lending for equipment should consider leasing as an alternative. They will need to evaluate the financial aspects and the legal and taxation framework to assess all of the costs associated with a lease, both for the institution and for their clients. Surveys with experienced clients can help to determine whether there is enough interest to justify the development and piloting of a microleasing product.

Government authorities should adopt a clear legal definition of financial leasing and treat leasing and lending equally under the tax codes. A standard definition of financial leasing should replace the broad array of definitions currently found in the various tax laws in Latin America, because a tax system that distinguishes between the two arrangements distorts the market.

As the experiences of the three Latin American MFIs demonstrate, the challenges to launching a leasing product are significant. The rewards for clients, however, can outweigh the initial costs of design and setup. Effective risk mitigation strategies limit the MFI's exposure and provide incentives for prompt repayment by clients holding leases. Given the proper market and legal and regulatory conditions, MFIs should consider adding leasing to the list of financial products they offer to existing and future clients.

---

8. See América Leasing, S.A., http://www.alsa.com.pe/index.html.

References

Fraslin, Jean-Hervé. 2003. "CECAM: A Cooperative Agricultural Financial Institution Providing Credit Adapted to Farmers' Demand in Madagascar." Case Study, International Association for Agricultural and Rural Credit–ICAR, U.S. Agency for International Development, Washington, DC, and World Council of Credit Unions, Inc., Madison, WI.

Goldberg, Michael. 2008. "Microleasing: Overcoming Equipment-Financing Barriers." *en Breve* 140: 3.

IADB (Inter-American Development Bank). 2009a. "Deepening the Bolivian Leasing Market." http://www.iadb.org/projects/loan.cfm?loan=ATN/ME-8989-BO.

———. 2009b. "Micro, Small, and Medium Enterprise." http://www.iadb.org/sds/mic/.

Westley, Glenn. 2003. *Arrendamiento y préstamo para equipo: Guía para el microfinanciamiento.* Washington, DC: Inter-American Development Bank.

———. 2007. "Préstamos y arrendamiento para equipo: Guía para las microfinanzas." Paper presented at a workshop at the World Bank, Washington, DC, October 17.

Additional Sources

Banking with the Poor Network. n.d. "Microleasing in Livelihood Restoration following a Natural Disaster," Brief 5, Banking with the Poor, Singapore.

Dowla, Asif Ud. 2004. "Microleasing: The Grameen Bank Experience." *Journal of Microfinance* 6 (2): 137–60.

Gutiérrez, Eduardo. 2007. "Micro leasing de ANED: Equipamos tu esfuerzo." Paper presented at a workshop for the World Bank, La Paz, October 17.

Moncada, Mario José. 2006. "A Push for Leasing." *La Prensa* (Managua), February 2.

Westley, Glenn. 2003. "Microleasing: The Unexplored Financing Instrument." *Microenterprise Development Review* 6 (1): 1–5.

7 DISASTER MANAGEMENT: PREPARING FOR THE WORST

I always tried to turn every disaster into an opportunity.

*John Rockefeller**

*John D. Rockefeller, quoted in ThinkExist.com Quotations, "John D. Rockefeller Quotes." http://thinkexist.com/quotation/i_always_tried_to_turn_every_disaster_into_an/13841.html (2010).

Natural disasters destroy the infrastructure that supports markets and provides basic needs. They wash out roads and tear out train lines. They bring down hospitals, schools, government buildings, and other basic health and human services infrastructure. They disable telecommunications, which become overloaded as frightened family and friends try to locate loved ones. No one escapes these impacts, but poor households and small businesses and microbusinesses are more directly and disproportionately affected.

This chapter presents the different kinds of costs incurred by disasters.[1] In addition, this discussion focuses on natural disaster preparation and how microfinance institutions (MFIs) and their staffs can respond. Preparation for disaster includes understanding the risks and costs of disasters, establishing proactive approaches and concrete responses, and knowing the additional resources and partnerships that may prove helpful in an emergency. Although they are often triggered by natural events, disasters are also the result of failures—failures of infrastructure, communications, financial services, and basic government services, among others. This chapter discusses the path to successful response to the failures made worse by natural disasters.

An Unfortunate but Common Story

Imagine the manager of a MFI arriving at the main office and finding windows smashed; the furniture, computers, and files destroyed; and the security system off-line. Even worse, most of the MFI's staff members fail to report to work, and the police condemn the office building as structurally unsafe. Is the manager prepared for such a situation? Will the MFI be able to continue offering its vital services when they are needed most?

This chaotic scene has been repeated worldwide—after earthquakes in El Salvador and Peru, hurricanes in Nicaragua and Guatemala, floods in Poland and Bangladesh, and the tsunami in South and Southeast Asia. If the MFI is like most such institutions around the world, it is completely unprepared for the destruction the manager finds—and the price to be paid by the MFI and its clients will be extraordinarily high.

Disasters can affect MFIs in physical, financial, and human ways. Aside from the physical destruction and human tragedy, disasters pose an enormous risk to the loan portfolio. For example, heavily subsidized or donated products—such as food and clothing from well-meaning donors—compete with the products from local microbusinesses. The affected microbusinesses cannot compete; they will lose potential sales and will be unable to make their loan repayment. This finding suggests a larger need for coordination as agencies and institutions come to the aid of disaster victims.

However, in the face of such tragedies, MFIs have proven that they can be important partners in preparation for disaster and postdisaster recovery efforts—thanks to their systems, products, and relationships with community leaders and microbusinesses. If they are prepared, MFIs can contribute to timely delivery of essential goods to affected neighborhoods. The MFIs may also need to respond with temporary changes in client selection processes and loan review policies; to new policies for using reserves; to changes in collecting, rescheduling, and refinancing; and even to a newly designed short-term loan product.

Costs of Disasters

The costs can be extraordinarily high. Damages from Hurricane Mitch in Nicaragua in 1998 amounted to about 45 percent of the national GDP. After the short-term destruction, the effects linger as tens of thousands

---

1. This chapter is based on the February 2008 dialogue with Enrique Pantoja (World Bank) and Mike Goldberg (World Bank).

are dislocated and need new short-term or long-term housing loans and income-generating opportunities, as well as productive assets. Table 7.1 shows a sampling of disasters, the affected countries, and the costs.

Table 7.1 **The Enormous Cost of Natural Disasters**

Event	Affected country or region	Costs
El Niño, 1999	Venezuela, R. B. de	30,000 dead from storms US$2 billion in damage
Earthquake, 2000	El Salvador	1,100 dead US$3 billion in damage
Tsunami, late 2004	India, Indonesia, Maldives, Sri Lanka	230,000 dead US$7 billion in damage
Hurricane season, 2005	Caribbean, Central America, Mexico (Yucatán peninsula)	4,100 dead 300,000 dislocated US$18 billion in damage
Earthquake, 2007	Peru	600 dead 300,000 dislocated US$0.9 billion in damage
Source: Authors.		

Human costs

The human costs are the most immediate. If they survive the tragedy, workers may lose their jobs and have to migrate in search of work. The MFI's managers, staff members, and their families may themselves be victims. The families left behind may find their homes destroyed or have no other source of housing, food, health care, or income to pay for those basic needs. In response, they may take their children out of school to work as day laborers. The community's main institutions that usually provide the services that address such basic needs—hospitals, markets, schools, daycare centers, police, fire stations, and the like—may also be unavailable.

In the wake of this devastation, the local MFI may be the best (or, perhaps, the only) source for immediate assistance. The nature of the clients' needs will be diverse. Each family and each business will have its own circumstance. Clients may come to the MFI's office urgently seeking cash—some or all of their savings or an emergency loan. They will need to meet urgent household needs, replace important assets, build up inventories of raw materials, repair equipment, or buy new animals.

Physical costs

Despite the great need for financial services, the physical destruction may prevent or hinder the MFI's ability to address its clients' needs. The MFI's physical infrastructure—the main office, branch offices, and the information systems—may be in immediate need of repair. Mobile phones, land line phones, and faxes may all be useless after a disaster. As a result, the MFI will be unable to update information on clients and loans; pay monthly bills; or make payments to commercial banks, donors, and other financing sources. Without a working infrastructure and the necessary information, the MFI will be unable to provide for its clients, or even manage the portfolio or its liabilities.

Financial costs

Financial costs for the MFI include liquidity effects, repayment issues, and changes in the priorities of commercial and other funders. Liquidity effects begin with the risk that the commercial banks holding the MFI's checking and savings accounts may suffer physical damage to facilities or may be overwhelmed by liquidity requirements. Borrowers may contribute to the MFI's liquidity problems by failing to pay on time. Even the best clients can face immediate problems in meeting repayment schedules. Displaced borrowers are in the worst position, because they will have to relocate their families and microbusinesses with no warning and may not be able to continue to use key productive assets or market locations. Eventually, the loss of neighborhood clients and walk-by traffic can be devastating to a business's cashflow and bottom line.

Because microbusinesses rarely have insurance coverage for income, assets, and health care needs, they may turn to the MFI to secure new loans or to reschedule or refinance existing loans that will cover losses and health costs. The spike in demand for loans from trusted clients also puts pressure on the MFI's liquidity. Decisions that affect the MFI's liquidity could have long-term repercussions for the MFI's reputation as a good partner to its clients, strategic allies, and investors.

If rescheduling or refinancing is permitted in the short term, MFIs should differentiate between those clients who performed well (with a reliable on-time repayment record) before the onset of the disaster and those who were already not living up to the loan contract agreement before the onset of the disaster. As soon as it is safe, loan officers should visit the affected neighborhoods to take stock of the situation for each of their clients. Loan officers may be in the best position to fine-tune the design of a short-term, relief-oriented loan product, because they know the cashflow capacity, creditworthiness, and character of each client or group of clients. The MFI should not consider a blanket refinancing policy, because this move would reward poor performers and could lead to a contagion effect later.

Inflation tends to spike after a natural disaster. This spike ripples through the economy, hurting microbusinesses, their suppliers, their clients, and the MFIs. Microbusinesses rarely maintain sufficient inventories to withstand interruptions in the supply of key inputs. Even if microbusinesses have built up inventories, given the quality of storage facilities, there is a strong likelihood of high losses in an emergency. Add the costs of replacing hand tools and simple machinery, and the microbusiness faces a daunting challenge—and may turn to the MFI for assistance.

The MFI may also have other financial burdens. Donors may divert programmatic funds to emergency relief efforts, leaving MFIs with a gap on the short-term liability side of the balance sheet. MFIs are expected to offer refinancing and rescheduling options to affected borrowers, in some cases creating a contagion effect (in other words, unaffected or marginally affected borrowers may expect similar options for extending loans or refinancing). The MFI may have to offer grace periods for new loans to trusted clients, with both significant liquidity and profitability implications in a context of worsening inflation. The MFI may be caught in a financial vice, thereby being trapped between inflationary pressures and a search for more expensive sources of financing on the one hand and slower repayment of the outstanding loans on the other.

Proactive Approaches and Concrete Responses

The opportunities and challenges for the MFI will change as the disaster cycle moves from relief to rehabilitation and long-term recovery. The study by Nagarajan (1998) of microfinance and disasters describes five stages in the cycle of disaster preparedness and response:

- Predisaster planning
- Immediate humanitarian relief
- The restoration of sustainable livelihoods
- The reconstruction of infrastructure
- Economic development and growth

How can MFIs respond effectively and efficiently to such disasters when the human, physical, and financial challenges are so overwhelming? Preparation and coordination between the various actors is the key. The MFI can assist its staff members, clients, local and national governments, and local and national aid agencies, especially in predisaster planning and during recovery (the first and fifth stages). As figure 7.1 shows, a four-stage framework on disaster risk management can help to visualize the stages of disaster preparedness and response by governments, MFIs, and other institutions.

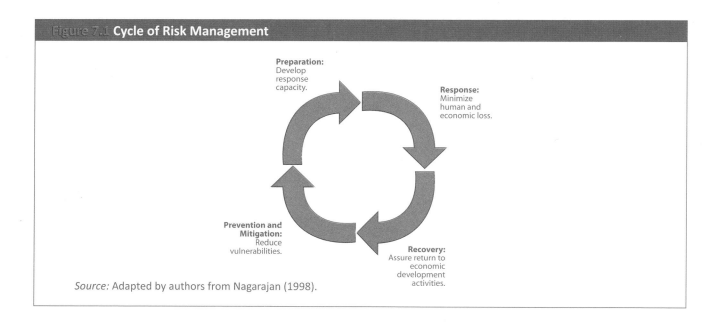

Figure 7.1 Cycle of Risk Management

Preparation: Develop response capacity.

Response: Minimize human and economic loss.

Prevention and Mitigation: Reduce vulnerabilities.

Recovery: Assure return to economic development activities.

Source: Adapted by authors from Nagarajan (1998).

Predisaster planning

Before disaster strikes, the MFI's management should develop a contingency plan. Given the losses that could result from the lack of preparation, the MFI board of directors may also wish to review the plan and provide inputs and help to establish emergency lending limitations and policies. The MFI's contingency plan should include policies for communications, management information systems, and human resources. For instance, a communications plan should govern exchanges between branches and headquarters staff. Clear instructions should be in place for backup systems as well. Critical information should be protected—with electronic backups of records maintained on a regular basis in a secure location outside the MFI's offices—if the MFI board considers this action to be prudent.

The MFI should conduct periodic reviews of its physical infrastructure and should update insurance policies to provide appropriate coverage of key facilities and assets. The contingency plan should include likely physical damage in headquarters, branches, and transportation links. Because insurance policies in many countries cover only specific types of damage and because they exclude "Acts of God," it is important to compare the policies, costs, and coverage of various providers.

Communication with clients is also important for the establishment of clear expectations of what support may be available in the aftermath of a disaster. The MFI can ensure adequate predisaster communication by preparing staff members. During the orientation provided to new clients, the MFI's staff can present disaster policies and practices. When clients apply for subsequent loans, the staff could briefly review the policies. If management decides that lending and collection policies will be more flexible in the event of a disaster, the staff should receive a special operating manual. This approach will ensure that all clients receive the same information about what assistance and adjustments are available.

Contingency funds

Because liquidity is often the biggest financial constraint after a disaster, the most direct approach to financial risk mitigation is a dedicated contingency fund. A contingency fund is an earmarked fund that may be accessed in times of disaster to help clients and MFIs survive and recover. Donors often help in disaster preparedness by establishing contingency funds, which comprise three types, differentiated by their organization and management. The first is assigned to a single MFI, usually a large institution with many years of experience, efficient administrative systems, and nationwide coverage. The second is operated by a special administrative unit. The third is shared by various MFIs: each one is responsible for regional coverage or specific communities. Contingency funds can be an advantageous solution for the clients, the MFI, the government, and the donors for five reasons:

- Clients can reestablish income streams quickly, thus getting funds for medicines, food, and temporary housing costs.
- When conditions return to normal, the MFI can reduce the risks of delinquent clients and loan loss reserves. Long-term client loyalty climbs when MFIs respond quickly to the client's emergency needs.
- The government may be overwhelmed by the disaster and may have to focus on the logistics of rescue, emergency housing, and massive relocation of communities. The MFI with a contingency fund can be an important ally in short-term recovery efforts.
- Donors often contribute to the initial capitalization of such funds, because contingency funds for disaster preparedness offer significant advantages to them as well.
- Administrative costs incurred by donors and local agencies decline and response time decreases when plans and contingency funds are in place.

Periodically, according to a strategic target, the MFI should add to a special reserve fund for disaster recovery. This earmarked fund can be used for disaster relief in the form of short-term loans to clients or as a recovery fund for the MFI (for example, to repair or replace key equipment and infrastructure).

Are disaster contingency funds appropriate for all situations? The most successful funds have been established in disaster-prone areas of South Asia. Larger MFIs are more likely to benefit from disaster contingency funds, because they are in a better position to make a strong case for using the resources efficiently and quickly. If the MFI can link to an existing contingency fund, such as a deferred drawdown option (DDO) that is established for disaster response (see box 7.1), then the reserves can be maintained at a minimum. However, in disaster-prone areas, it would be wise to always have such funds waiting for the next round of claims. The example of Buro-Tangail (box 7.2) shows how contingency funds can be used for a number of purposes, while being ready for disasters.

Box 7.1 Catastrophe Risk DDO

The World Bank Group is offering a new financial product, the catastrophe risk DDO (CAT DDO), to governments of middle-income countries. Similar to a line of credit, the product is designed for countries that have no immediate need for funds but that might need them if unforeseen events make it difficult to access the capital markets. In this case, the purpose is to make financing immediately available after a natural disaster. The CAT DDO is intended to fill the gap while other sources of funding, such as emergency relief aid, are being mobilized. A government can access funds from the facility if it declares a state of emergency as a result of a natural disaster. Countries that sign up for the CAT DDO must have an adequate hazard risk management program in place. The maximum amount available will be US$500 million or 0.25 percent of a country's GDP, whichever is smaller. The funds may be drawn down over a three-year period, which may be renewed up to four times for a total of 15 years. The CAT DDO allows countries to defer disbursements for up to three years and, upon renewal, for another three years.

The new policy addresses certain disincentives to using the option. The revisions ensure that borrowers will have greater certainty of availability of funds because the World Bank will continuously monitor the borrower's economy to allow disbursement upon request. The funds may be drawn down at any time, unless the Bank gives prior notification to the borrower that one or more of the drawdown conditions have not been met. In addition, the CAT DDO's revised pricing eliminates the commitment fee and surcharge for the longer maturity and is thus aligned with standard International Bank for Reconstruction and Development terms.

Source: Adapted by authors from World Bank (2008).

Box 7.2 Buro-Tangail Contingency Fund, Bangladesh

The Buro-Tangail Fund in Bangladesh has been a pioneer in disaster planning. While its contingency fund is ready for emergencies, those reserves also help the institution to deal with smaller challenges. If a borrower dies or becomes permanently incapacitated, the fund can be used to cancel the outstanding debt. Also, the fund can be used to provide supplemental loans to borrowers when their productive assets are damaged or stolen. Finally, when a loan is more than six months overdue, the reserve fund can be applied to the balance.

Source: Adapted by authors from Nagarajan (1998).

There are also regional and international mechanisms for immediate financial responses to some types of disasters. Six governments in the Caribbean have signed a DDO loan with the World Bank, with open credit lines in the case of a disaster that reaches a certain magnitude (such as hurricanes classified above a certain category). Such facilities ensure immediate access to Bank funds in the event of a disaster, at a low cost to the government (see box 7.3). MFIs could investigate whether such liquidity and risk management options could cover their clients' short-term needs as well. The Bank and governments in Central and South America are already discussing how to set up similar multicountry risk management and liquidity systems.

> **Box 7.3 Loan Product Adjustments for Disasters: The Case of the Bangladesh Rural Advancement Committee (BRAC)**
>
> Because of the monsoon season and the country's huge delta basin, floods are a regular threat to the productive assets of Bangladesh's microbusinesses. Several MFIs have developed financial products that address this risk. One industry leader, BRAC, has made specific adjustments in the following loan policies and credit characteristics to deal with disaster situations:
>
> - Clients can withdraw savings up to a specific preestablished amount.
> - Regular loan repayments can be suspended for a period.
> - Interest rates can be reduced significantly for up to two months.
> - Loans can be restructured for clients with marginal disaster losses (based on field visits).
> - Loans can be refinanced for clients with high disaster losses (based on field visits).
> - New loans are offered for productive asset replacement of up to 12 months at 15 percent interest.
> - An option of disbursement in the form of seeds, animals, and other in-kind materials is available.
>
> *Source:* Adapted by Enrique Pantoja from BRAC materials.

Immediate humanitarian relief

At this stage, the MFI can play the role of facilitator, putting municipal and Government officials in touch with microbusinesses and community leaders. The MFI can lend some of its facilities to the relief effort, including vehicles, staff, and buildings. If MFI staff members have received the necessary training, they can also assist in disaster assessments.

Restoration of livelihoods. The MFI should have clear, well-defined policies in place concerning the types of temporary loans to be provided—consumer loans, housing repair loans, and working capital loans. Extended grace periods can help microbusinesses recover more quickly. The MFI may use previous loan repayment performance as one way to prioritize which business operators receive the special business recovery loans. The MFI may also ask the communities to back a recovery loan with a character reference.

Branch offices should be trained to respond to requests for emergency loans by clients and others in affected areas. Management should establish specific lending limits for clients, new client selection criteria, and possibly adjustments to collateral and other normal requirements. Management should provide the disaster relief guidelines in internal written communications, in case branch office staff members are unable to contact the headquarters office. When branch managers know what levels of lending authority and special loan conditions apply in an emergency, they are better prepared to act independently to respond to clients' needs during such times.

The 1997 floods in Poland provide an innovative example of disaster management and the successful use of an MFI loan product to restore livelihoods. Floods from four rivers had severely affected 1,400 small towns, thereby destroying 50,000 homes, forcing the relocation of 160,000 people, and causing US$4 billion of damage. Given its national coverage, the MFI Fundusz Mikro was asked to manage a special disaster recovery fund. Fundusz Mikro opened a special lending window within its branches, thus developing a new brand and loan product just for the emergency situation. This product had a different contract format and lending terms (a 24-month loan term, a 10 percent near-commercial interest rate, and a 6-month grace period). Even the delivery mechanism was adjusted, with a special window for processing loan applications.

Existing and new clients formed solidarity groups of five members, evaluated the damage, and submitted loan applications. The solidarity group was responsible for assigning priorities to members with urgent needs. Fundusz Mikro disbursed the loan, monitored business performance, and collected the payment. Loan recovery was assisted by local municipalities. Because this change was a one-time contingency fund approach, there was no capitalization of the fund.

By the end of the six-month emergency period, Fundusz Mikro had not only responded to the unique set of circumstances, but also identified a significant number of new clients for a postdisaster long-term commercial relationship. By setting a time limit on the emergency loan product, Fundusz Mikro was able to maintain credit discipline, while building a reputation as a socially responsible MFI. Finally, with on-time repayment of 93 percent, Fundusz Mikro was able to demonstrate that, even under the most difficult conditions, its client selection methodology was sound.

Some MFIs in Latin America have prepared for and responded well to disasters, including earthquakes and floods caused by hurricanes. Examples include Katalysis and its Central American partners after Hurricane Mitch's devastation in 1998 (see box 7.4) and housing loans by the Association of Micro, Small, and Medium Development Consultants (Asociación de Consultores para el Desarrollo de la Pequeña, Mediana, y Microempresa, or ACODEP) in Nicaragua. Katalysis, a U.S.-based nongovernmental organization with a network of Central American MFIs, gained valuable experience in the wake of Hurricane Mitch's destruction. The focus on preparedness led to simple guidelines that were shared with member MFIs. Some of the instructions included (1) continually backing up loan data; (2) building a disaster fund using a small share of interest earned on loans; and (3) maintaining a disaster supplies kit, including a generator, first-aid kits, and transistor radios.

ACODEP has been a leading MFI in Nicaragua for 20 years. In response to several disasters affecting clients, ACODEP developed a housing product called "mi vivienda." After Hurricane Mitch, ACODEP provided more than 2,000 loans for rebuilding homes, which often included microbusiness workshops. The loan typically covered building materials, with the client's sweat equity. In some cases, ACODEP has lent to clients for their relocation and building of a home outside hazard-prone areas.

Box 7.4 Katalysis: Response to Disasters

In response to the personal, economic, and financial disaster that followed Hurricane Mitch, Katalysis, a U.S.-based NGO, implemented the following special loan management policies:

1. Suspend the collection of interest and principal for a short time in major disasters.
2. Allow the most affected clients to withdraw savings without a penalty.
3. Do not provide new loans until the MFI has fully analyzed the impact of the crisis.
4. Provide refinancing for only the most affected clients.
5. Develop new products, such as housing loans, to respond to damage to clients' homes.
6. In general, do not forgive loans (thereby maintaining the MFI's image as a professional financial institution). However, forgive the loan balances for clients who have died.

Source: Adapted by authors from Woodworth (2006) and Hildebrand (2002).

As the examples of the Bangladesh Rural Advancement Committee, Fundusz Mikro, and ACODEP show, beyond the adjustments to existing products, MFIs can launch new products to address some specific disaster-related impacts. Those new products can build client loyalty and minimize the response time to client requests. Such products include emergency loans, housing loans, cereal banks, remittance services, and subsistence loans (see table 7.2).

Table 7.2 New Financial Products, Results, and Implications

Financial Product	Results	Implications
Emergency loans	Increased client loyalty occurs. Good repayment is recorded only with existing clients.	Loans are effective only during relief stages. Partial safely net is provided for existing clients.
Housing loans	Moderate repayment occurs. Timely loans based on demand and flexible terms and conditions are rare. Loans are made only to those who owned houses prior to a disaster.	Loans are effective only when issued quickly during rehabilitation and when reconstruction stages are based on demand.
Remittance services	Services ease cashflow problems of clients and increase repayments. Client loyalty to MFI increases.	Services are required immediately after disaster up to reconstruction stages. A quicker return to normalcy is facilitated. Use should be demand based.
Subsistence loans for disaster preparedness	Loans are required for buying and storing subsistence goods during emergency stages and result in good repayments and increased client loyalty.	Partial safety net for clients is provided. Loans are effective with only trusted long-term clients.

Source: Adapted by authors from Nagarajan (1998).

Restoration of sustainable livelihoods and assets. This is the most important time in the recovery cycle for MFIs, because they can play a fundamental role in assisting the recovery of microbusinesses. If predisaster planning has been effective, many decisions on clients, loans, and procedures will already be in place. However, it is helpful to discuss the types of products that might be of most use to clients as the livelihood restoration process begins and as the stock of productive assets is rebuilt.

There are also important implications for the types of products and delivery mechanisms following a disaster. MFIs have responded with new policies for existing products and even new loan products for limited periods. When new policies are put in place, they are related to client selection, contract enforcement, funds management, delivery methodology, and additional complementary services. For example, if the MFI provides emergency housing loans, it may be more efficient to make arrangements with large wholesalers of construction materials, warehouses, and delivery companies to get better prices and to pay the supplier directly in the name of clients. In other words, it may be sensible for the MFI to provide products it would usually avoid, like in-kind loans or limited loan rescheduling.

Conclusion

This chapter has shown the broad repercussions and huge costs of a disaster. Experts have identified five stages of disaster preparedness and recovery. Whether they are slow onset or instantaneous shocks, disasters can have devastating effects on all aspects of a society and the economy. For this reason, disaster preparedness can save lives and property and can speed the process of recovery.

Governments, donors, and MFIs have important roles to play to speed relief and begin the recovery process. Governments coordinate efforts from disaster preparedness to the moment the damage reports arrive, as well as through midterm recovery. Donors often respond by establishing contingency funds that are dedicated to financing recovery efforts. MFIs have a unique combination of skills, networks, and client bases that make them valuable partners, from the initial onset to the sustained recovery after a disaster.

By coordinating with other MFIs, government agencies, municipal authorities, and donors, the MFI is in a strong position to be an important partner in local, regional, and even national responses. With plans in place for the most likely human, physical, and financial shocks in the aftermath of a hurricane, earthquake, or flood, the MFI can serve the immediate needs of its clients. Some effective responses to disasters have included new types of loan products, adjustments to conditions for outstanding loans, and changes in delivery methodologies (such as allowing groups to set lending priorities among members). Whatever the response, MFIs should learn from the painful lessons of the past—because the benefits of preparing for the next disaster far outweigh the costs.

References

Hildebrand, Jerry. 2002. Presentation at the Annual Microenterprise Conference, Katalysis, Brigham Young University, Provo, UT.

Nagarajan, Geetha. 1998. *Microfinance in the Wake of Natural Disasters: Challenges and Opportunities. Microenterprise Best Practices.* Washington, DC: World Bank.

Woodworth, Warner. 2006. *Microcredit in Post-Conflict, Conflict, Natural Disaster, and Other Difficult Settings.* Salt Lake City, UT: Brigham Young University Marriott School.

World Bank. 2008. "Background Note: Catastrophe Risk Deferred Drawdown Option (DDO), or CAT DDO." http://web.worldbank.org/WBSITE/EXTERNAL/NEWS/0,,contentMDK:21670477~pagePK:6425 7043~piPK:437376~theSitePK:4607,00.html.

Additional Sources

Goldberg, Michael. 2008. "Cómo se puede proteger clientes e IMFs después de desastres?" Paper presented at a workshop at the World Bank, Washington, DC, February 13.

Katalysis. 2001. "When Disaster Strikes: An Action Plan for Preparation and Response for the Unexpected in Central America." Katalysis Partnership, Stockton, CA.

Mathison, Stuart, ed. 2003. *Microfinance and Disaster Management.* Brisbane, Australia: Foundation for Development Cooperation.

Nagarajan, Geetha. 2006. "Microfinance and Cash-for-Work in Livelihood Restoration following a Natural Disaster." Brief 4, Banking with the Poor Network, Singapore.

Pantoja, Enrique. 2008. "Microfinanzas y la gestión del riesgo a desastres naturales." Paper presented at a workshop at the World Bank, Washington, DC, February 13.

8 New Technologies: Providing a Path to Lower Costs and New Products

Information technology and business are becoming inextricably interwoven.

*Bill Gates**

*Bill Gates, quoted in "Woopidoo Business and Finance Quotes." http://www.woopidoo.com/business_quotes/authors/bill-gates-quotes.htm (2010).

Introduction

In rapidly evolving financial markets, applied technologies can be the difference between a larger share of the market or a gradual decline. Sustainable microfinance institutions (MFIs) can use technology to reach a large scale of operations and can offer services to tens of thousands, even millions, of clients. With cost-effective technological solutions that meet their data management needs and match their clients' requirements, those MFIs can cover their operating and financial costs and the risk of loan losses without the need for subsidies.

This chapter explores some of the technological innovations that MFIs are using to improve service and to expand access to their clients.[1] The chapter describes innovations in mobile banking, in network systems, and in the emerging technology of biometrics. The chapter also discusses the substantial costs, risks, and challenges of achieving effective technology adoption at the institutional and policy levels, and it offers guidance to MFI practitioners and policy makers about how to approach and foster technological innovations in microfinance.

Why Technology Matters

Microfinance is a business of scale. Therefore, it is highly sensitive to variable costs. Even a few pennies of savings per client matter when the MFI is serving tens of thousands of clients with short-term loans, savings collection, and other financial products. Passing the savings on to clients helps MFIs reach their social objectives. In other words, returns on technology investments that lower operational costs for MFIs can be very high, thus benefitting tens of thousands of clients.

The fastest way to lower variable costs is to adopt new technologies that speed the analysis of client data, to lower transaction costs, and to make it easier for clients to use microloans effectively. The key hardware and software needed to apply new technologies to microfinance are already in place, especially point-of-sale (POS) and mobile phone systems, as figure 8.1 illustrates.

---

1. This paper is based on the August 2007 dialogue with Hannah Siedek (Consultative Group to Assist the Poor), Alice Lui (Development Alternatives, Inc.), and Santiago Saavedra (Red Transaccional Cooperativa).

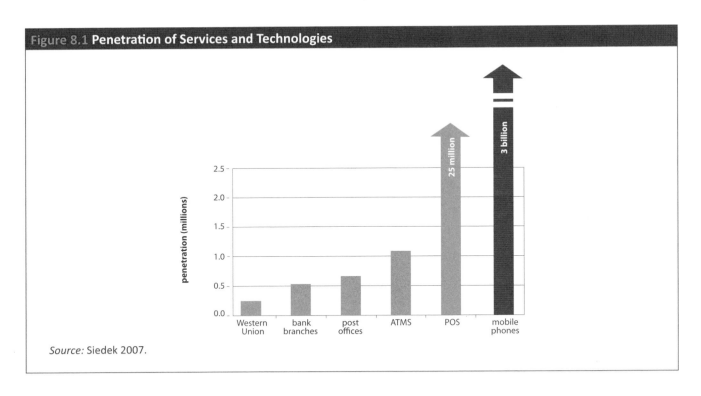

Figure 8.1 Penetration of Services and Technologies

Source: Siedek 2007.

Mobile Banking

The advent of mobile phone payment technologies—whereby users can receive and transfer value in small amounts through the mobile phone network—has the potential to revolutionize access to financial services. As table 8.1 reveals, mobile phone penetration is a worldwide phenomenon. Beyond standard communication services, mobile phones offer four characteristics that directly affect banking transactions: (1) fast message transmission speed, (2) a high degree of reliability, (3) low costs, and (4) security.

Whereas only about 25 percent of all households in developing countries have formal relationships with banks, more than 40 percent use mobile phones, and that number continues to grow rapidly. More than 1 billion people without formal banking relationships already have mobile phones. India had 370 million active mobile phone cards for connections (known as subscriber identity modules, or SIMs) at the end of January 2009 and is adding about 15 million per month. Pakistan has about 90 million connections and is adding 2 million per month (ITU 2009; Mas and Kumar 2008; Mas and Siedek 2008).

Table 8.1 Wireless Penetration Rates, 2003–12

Region	2003	2008	2012 (estimated)
Africa	4.7	30.6	50.1
Asia and Pacific	13.1	39.1	60.8
Eastern Europe	20.5	102.8	134.7
Latin America	19.7	70.4	90.8
Middle East	17.8	61.9	98.3
Source: Mas and Kumar 2008.			

Mobile banking still faces important challenges—from the perspective of technology development to operator skills and client perceptions. Practical issues with mobile phones include small screens, tiny keyboards, limited connectivity, and unreliable connections in remote areas. Operators control the security of the system and must cope with unreliable wireless connections from remote areas. Their interaction with wary clients can be the difference between rejection and technology adoption on a large scale. Clients are typically resistant to new technologies and may be especially reluctant to trust their funds to a wireless system. However, client education efforts can help to overcome such concerns. Those operational problems do not limit the potential for a broad microfinance revolution (covering loans, savings, payments, and remittances) through mobile phones.

The Philippines' financial sector, for example, has been a leader in leveraging mobile phones and networks to deliver cost-effective, high-volume, low-value transfer capabilities. Two of the country's mobile network operators offer the functional equivalent of small-scale transaction banking to an estimated 5.5 million customers (Lyman, Pickens, and Porteous 2008). One service provider, Globe Telecom, has partnered with the Rural Bankers Association of the Philippines to offer its "GCash" service, which enables customers to use text messaging to repay loans and to make deposits, withdrawals, or transfers from their savings account, thereby using the network of GCash agents to deposit or withdraw cash.

The Wizzit Bank in South Africa is another promising example of the use of mobile phones to transfer value to and from a financial intermediary. In 2002, Wizzit was conceived as a virtual commercial bank relying heavily on mobile phones—there are no buildings or branch offices (Ivatury and Pickens 2006a). Wizzit allied itself to the South African Bank of Athens to secure a banking license, and it began operations in 2005. Customers can use their mobile phones, automated teller machines (ATM), POS terminals, and offices in the South African Bank of Athens to make deposits, withdrawals, loan payments, transfers between accounts, and international and domestic remittances and to effect payments for goods and services. As of January 2009, Wizzit had 250,000 customers who are able to deposit and withdraw cash through their mobile phones (Lapper 2009). Through an alliance with Beehive, a rural MFI, Wizzit is also expanding to provide services to clients in more remote rural areas.

Network Systems

POS terminals are often part of a network that is shared by financial intermediaries; clients from a number of institutions can use the same terminals and agents to make payments. Sharing network infrastructure enables financial institutions to achieve collectively the volume of transactions needed to cover the costs of the software, hardware, and the connectivity required to provide distributed payments services. Some MFIs, particularly in the cooperatives sector, are working together to create economies of scale that enable them to reduce costs and to expand services by investing in new payment technologies.

The Red Transaccional Cooperativa (also known as Red Coonecta), is a credit cooperative network formed in 2006 in Ecuador with help from the World Council of Credit Unions (Saavedra 2007). The high cost of setting up an office had limited the expansion of cooperatives. In addition, strong competition from commercial banks limited the ability of the small MFIs to expand their portfolios. In response, the cooperatives decided to establish a network to facilitate members' nationwide access to services. The goal of the council's support was to use technology to integrate as many cooperatives as possible and to provide access to new service delivery technologies.

The growth of the network has been impressive. During the first 16 months (through August 2007), the network incorporated one agency per week and developed a network of 153 offices and 15 financial cooperatives (about one-third of the financial cooperatives in the country). The services currently offered by the Red Coonecta to its members include a network of shared branch offices, a POS network, debit cards, remittance distribution, and payment of public utility services. The network was recently integrated into the national ATM network as well, with more than 2,000 machines across the country. As a result, a member of a cooperative can use any ATM in the country to obtain funds, make deposits, and check transactions. Red Coonecta has recently expanded to include service links with national and international networks—with neighboring countries and the Credit Union Service Corporation of the United States. This U.S. connection facilitates sending remittances from immigrants in the United States to family members in Ecuador.

Remote Data Processing

From Mexico to India, MFIs use mobile devices—personal digital assistants (PDAs), smart phones, and laptops—to analyze a client's risk and to determine creditworthiness in the field. Those improvements can result in important reductions in paperwork and the time to deliver the loans and can improve client selection. Setup and operating costs are low, with software development ranging from US$20,000 to US$80,000. Hardware costs are around US$100 per unit, and annual software maintenance contracts are less than US$10,000.

The use of mobile applications represents a savings to clients, because they may not have to leave their place of business to apply for or receive a loan. It also means that loans officers are more productive in terms of the number of clients they can serve and the quality of their loans. The evaluation and approval of a credit application, for example, requires detailed information on the client, the business, the family members, and other relevant aspects of the operation. Using a mobile device, the loan officer can enter information directly into the system and can reduce the number of errors or incomplete applications. Optimally, loan officers can also access all prior information on a client and can run credit scoring programs on existing clients with new loans and on new clients, oftentimes generating a credit decision on the spot.

PDAs

PDAs can help MFIs to standardize lending methodologies, to lower transaction times, to improve loan officer efficiency, and to increase data accuracy. PDAs have been used by ADOPEM (Dominican Republic), SKS Microfinance (India), BanGente (República Bolivariana de Venezuela), Banco Solidario (Ecuador), and Compartamos and Fincomun (both in Mexico).

One of the early adopters of PDA technology for microfinance applications was Compartamos, a specialized microfinance provider using village banking for female clients in Mexico. Compartamos found that PDAs raised loan officer efficiency and data access in the field (Waterfield 2004). The example of Compartamos, however, reveals a potential problem with early adoption of new technology. That is, the efficiency of using PDAs can be sustained only if the overall management information system (MIS) is stable, if it permits high-speed data transfer between branches for consolidation, and if it has ongoing technical support. As a result of software development issues and MIS-PDA interface problems, Compartamos later suspended the use of PDAs. The Compartamos example also suggests that PDAs require mature loan products to avoid constant adjustments because loan specifications and data requirements change over time.

However, for Banco Solidario in Ecuador, using PDAs has resulted in significant improvements in productivity and efficiency. During the first 10 months that loan officers used PDAs, the loan portfolio grew from less than US$2 million to almost US$10 million, as figure 8.2 demonstrates. There was a direct correlation between the use of PDAs and the drop in problematic loans. PDAs may also help to reduce the level of risk in the loan portfolio and, as a result, may improve the institution's risk management (see figure 8.3).

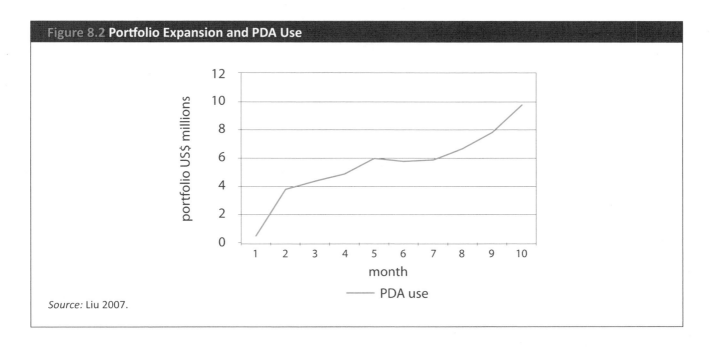

Figure 8.2 **Portfolio Expansion and PDA Use**

Source: Liu 2007.

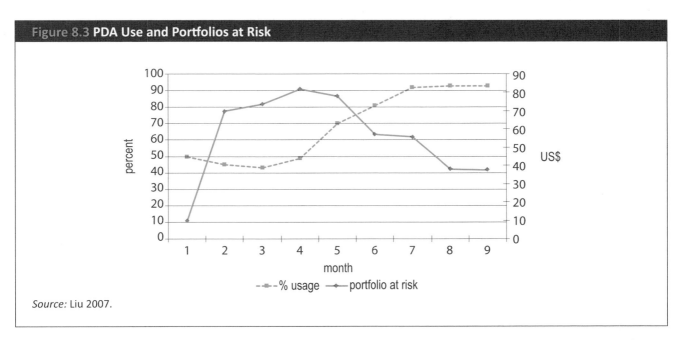

Figure 8.3 **PDA Use and Portfolios at Risk**

Source: Liu 2007.

POS Terminals

The mobile phone is one interface to the banking system. It requires high penetration rates and reliable, well-connected networks to be effective. POS terminals are another potentially very efficient means to effect low-value transactions in a highly distributed manner. POS terminals generally use card swipe technology, bar code readers, and modems to transmit data from debit or credit cards to financial intermediaries, thus enabling financial transactions or the sale of products or services. The minimum specifications for POS terminals are outlined in box 8.1.

Box 8.1 Minimum Requirements for a POS Device

A POS device requires the following minimum specifications:

- A card reader that can read the information stored on the magnetic stripe or chip of a card (The reader also may be able to write information into the chip, if it is off line and the card is virtual—that is, embedded in a mobile phone.)
- A numeric keypad, through which users can enter their personal identification number and transaction amounts
- A screen large enough for the users to view and to validate information pertaining to the transaction
- A set of encryption keys held in highly secure memory, with all communications between the POS terminal and the bank's server conveyed securely—with no possibility of decryption by a third party (The standard is keys of a minimum length of 128 bits.)
- A printer to issue receipts for each (successful or attempted) transaction

Source: Adapted by authors from Mas and Siedek (2008).

POS partners may include supermarkets, pharmacies, gas stations, post offices, or other businesses that have reliable access to communications networks and contact with the target audience. Agents must be selected carefully, however, because they are (1) providing customer service for the financial intermediary, (2) carrying an MFI's transactions on their own balance sheet while funds are settled, and (3) intermediating what may be large sums of cash between clients and institutions. The client's trust must be ensured for effective intermediation. For that reason, a strong client orientation and clear understanding of client needs and limitations are requisites for effective representation of a MFI.

MFIs have successfully developed and leveraged large networks of POS agents in Brazil, Colombia, Kenya, Maldives, Mongolia, Pakistan, and the Philippines, among others.[2] In Brazil, banks have partnered with more than 95,000 local merchants, post offices, and lottery dealers equipped with POS terminals to offer financial services in 1,600 municipalities that previously had little or no bank presence (Mas and Siedek 2008).

Biometrics

Biometrics refers to the measuring of a person's unique physical characteristics, like fingerprints or facial features, to verify identity. The technology records the clients' biometric features—fingerprints are most commonly used—and stores this information on the MFI's database and, usually, on a smart card the client carries for transactions (Whelan 2003).

Biometric readers can be installed on ATM machines (creating biometric ATMs, or BTMs) and on handheld devices, so clients can verify their identities by simply touching (in the case of fingerprints) the reader's scanner.

---

2. See Consultative Group to Assist the Poor, http://www.cgap.org/p/site/c/tech/, and Barton and others (2007).

The scanned image is then compared to the client's recorded biometric feature, either located on the client's smart card or accessed through a network connected to the MFI's servers. Authentication is guaranteed when the scanned image matches the original biometric feature.

Biometric solutions enable clients and MFIs to conduct secure transactions remotely, because they reduce the need for staff members to be present. When they replace signatures, biometrics can also significantly cut down on the paper records that must be processed and archived, which is often one of the most labor-intensive components of information management. Biometrics work better than signatures because they are nearly impossible to forge. They provide a secure means even for illiterate clients to authorize a transaction. Biometric technology also has an advantage over passwords and personal identification numbers, which are easily forgotten or can be transferred from person to person. Biometric and smart card technologies have been deployed in Indonesia's PT Bank Danamon, India's ICICI Bank, and Bolivia's Prodem Fondo Financiero Privado (FFP), which have also reportedly lowered the costs of administering high-volume, low-value microfinance transactions (Yeo 2008).

The case of Prodem FFP in Bolivia illustrates the potential of biometrics to reduce costs and to increase the security of microfinance transactions. Prodem FFP first introduced its biometric solution in 2000, writing its own software to integrate the biometric readers and smart cards with its MIS. At Prodem FFP's 54 branch offices, computers were equipped with card readers and fingerprint scanners. Tellers were able to verify customer identity more quickly and to speed up transaction times. BTMs have also been set up at many Prodem FFP offices so clients can securely conduct savings, transfer, and loan disbursements without having to wait for a teller.[3]

Costs, Risks, and Challenges

Implementing new technologies can be hugely rewarding to MFIs and their clients, but they are often very costly, risky, and disruptive to the institution. Those challenges occur whenever new technologies are introduced in financial intermediation. Managing a successful technology implementation program requires careful planning and attention to many factors. Management will need to determine the specific objectives of a technology project, to assess the variables that will drive costs and benefits, and to evaluate whether the project is likely to pay off. In addition to the upfront hardware and software costs, the costs of training, maintenance, and upgrades must be included in the planning.

Before deciding to adopt new information and communications technology, the MFI should examine its goals and should evaluate the state and use of its existing systems. If the management expects to reengineer the entire system, a phased approach is usually best. For example, innovative solutions for loan processing and payments distribution require a robust MIS. Learning how to analyze the information coming from that system and how to apply it to business decisions is often a big institutional challenge itself.[4]

To assess a technology project's return on investment, MFIs must pay close attention to the costs and benefits they accrue on a transactional basis. Oftentimes, technology investments in microfinance require large economies of scale to become viable. Given the volume of expected transactions or the average amount of each transaction, the communications cost of authorizing payments over land line, mobile phone, or broadband networks, for example, may be too high to justify the costs of a POS network. In regions with low population density or low

---

3. The information presented on the Prodem FFP case study comes from Whelan (2003), with contributions from the staff of Consultative Group to Assist the Poor and from eChange, LLC.
4. For resources on planning and implementing technology projects, see Progressive Technology Project (2009) and TechSoup (2009).

References

Barton, Susana, Carlos del Busto, Christian Rodriguez, and Alice Liu. 2007. "Client-Focused MFI Technologies Case Study." microReport 77, U.S. Agency for International Development, Washington, DC.

ITU (International Telecommunication Union). 2009. *Measuring the Information Society: The ICT Development Index.* Geneva: ITU.

Ivatury, Guatam, and Nicole Pasricha. 2005. "Funding Microfinance Technology." Donor Brief 23, Consultative Group to Assist the Poor, Washington, DC.

Ivatury, Guatam, and Mark Pickens. 2006a. "Mobile Phone Banking and Low-Income Customers: Evidence from South Africa." Consultative Group to Assist the Poor, World Bank, and United Nations Foundation, Washington, DC.

———. 2006b. "Mobile Phones for Microfinance." Brief, Consultative Group to Assist the Poor, Washington, DC.

Lapper, Richard. 2009. "A Call to South Africa's Masses." *Financial Times*, January 7.

Liu, Alice. 2007. "Client-Focused MFI Technologies: Case Study." Paper presented at a workshop at the World Bank, Washington, DC, August 15.

Lyman, Timothy, Mark Pickens, and David Porteous. 2008. "Regulating Transformational Branchless Banking: Mobile Phones and Other Technology to Increase Access to Finance." Focus Note 43, Consultative Group to Assist the Poor, Washington, DC.

Mas, Ignacio, and Kabir Kumar. 2008. "Banking on Mobiles: Why, How, for Whom?" Focus Note 48, Consultative Group to Assist the Poor, Washington, DC.

Mas, Ignacio, and Hannah Siedek. 2008. "Banking through Networks of Retail Agents." Focus Note 47, Consultative Group to Assist the Poor, Washington, DC.

Progressive Technology Project. 2009. "Tech Assistance Resources." http://progressivetech.org/tech-assistance-resources.

Saavedra, Santiago. 2007. "Red Transaccional del Ecuador." Paper presented at a workshop at the World Bank, Washington, DC, August 15.

Siedek, Hannah. 2007. "CGAP Programa de tecnologia: Una incubadora para la innovación." Paper presented at a workshop at the World Bank, Washington, DC, August 15.

TechSoup. 2009. "Technology." http://www.techsoup.org/learningcenter/techplan/index.cfm.

Waterfield, Charles. 2004. "Personal Digital Assistants." IT Innovation Series, Consultative Group to Assist the Poor, Washington, DC.

Whelan, Steve. 2003. "Biometrics Technology." IT Innovation Series, Consultative Group to Assist the Poor, Washington, DC.

Yeo, Vivian. 2008. "Asian Banks Look to Smart Cards for Microfinance Boost." *Business Week*, January 8.

Additional Sources

Consultative Group to Assist the Poor. http://www.cgap.org.

Lyman, Timothy R., Gautam Ivatury, and Stefan Staschen. 2006. "Empleo de agentes en la banca sin sucursales para los pobres." Focus Note 38, Consultative Group to Assist the Poor, Washington, DC.

Technology Resource Group. http://www.techrg.com/.

Wright, Graham, Nick Hughes, Brian Richardson, and David Cracknell. 2006. "Mobile Phone-Based E-Banking: The Customer Value Proposition." Briefing Note 47, MicroSave, Nairobi, Kenya.

Glossary

Access to finance—Access to finance is the ease with which businesses and households are able to qualify for and get credit and other financial services in a timely and reliable manner and at an affordable cost. For example, access to finance by poor people can be affected directly by the level of collateral and documentation required for loans, by the formal presentation of a business use of the funds, and by minimum balance requirements for savings accounts.

Assembly or general assembly—This governing body is used by some nongovernmental organizations (NGOs) to select, appoint, or approve members of the board of directors. In some cases, the assembly may be a representative body elected by members of the NGO. In other cases, each NGO member may have its own voice on the general assembly.

Biometrics—Biometrics is the measuring of a person's unique physical characteristics, such as fingerprints or facial features, to verify identity. The technology records the clients' biometric features—fingerprints are the most commonly use—and stores this information on the MFI's database and, usually, on a smart card that the client carries for transactions.

Board of directors—A board is a group of individuals elected or appointed to establish institutional management policies and to make decisions on major issues. In NGOs, the board is often elected by the general assembly or appointed by NGO founders. In shareholder-owned institutions, the board is elected by shareholders.

Deferred drawdown option—A deferred drawdown option (DDO) allows a country borrowing funds from the World Bank to postpone disbursement of a loan for a defined period, instead of drawing down funds immediately after approval. A catastrophe risk DDO (CAT DDO) provides liquidity immediately following a natural disaster which results in a declaration of a state of emergency.

Financial lease—Under the terms of a financial lease, the client pays the full price of the equipment, plus interest, in installment payments throughout the lease period. At the end of the lease period, the client may purchase the equipment outright for a nominal amount (usually the remainder of the asset's cost).

Institutional shareholders—Shareholders are persons or entities that own shares or equity in a microfinance institution (MFI). Shareholders may include individual private investors, NGOs, or other institutional investors. In credit unions, shareholders are commonly referred to as members.

Institutional stakeholders—Stakeholders represent owner and nonowner groups with a legitimate interest in the company's performance and with influence that might have a positive or negative effect on a company's commercial performance and long-term sustainability. Stakeholders include regulators, providers of financing, employees, clients, and the larger community.

Management information system—A management information system (MIS) is the system of collecting, archiving, retrieving, and using information. In microfinance, the MIS tracks loan officer productivity and clients' repayments schedules and balances, among others. A good information system is vital for making timely assessments of the quality of the loan portfolio and other variables that most affect cost and risk.

Microcredit—Microcredit is the provision of loans tailored to the needs and capacity of microbusinesses and low-income households. Institutions providing microcredit are usually prohibited by national laws from mobilizing savings or providing other financial services beyond credit.

Microfinance—Microfinance is the provision of basic financial services (such as loans, savings, money transfers, and microinsurance) to microbusinesses and poor people. People living in poverty, like everyone else, need a diverse range of financial services to run their businesses, to build assets, to smooth consumption, and to manage risks. (See Consultative Group to Assist the Poor, http://www.cgap.org).

Microfinance institutions—MFIs are financial intermediaries that offer specialized products (such as loans, savings, and payment services) that match the needs and capacity of low-income households and microbusinesses. Some are regulated, supervised financial institutions (such as banks and credit unions) while others are more informal (such as rotating savings and credit associations, village banks, and nongovernment microcredit institutions).

Microinsurance—Insurance is "a risk management system under which individuals, businesses, and other organizations or entities, in exchange for payment of a sum of money (a premium), offer an opportunity to share the risk of possible financial loss through guaranteed compensation for losses resulting from certain perils under specified conditions." (http://www.microfinancerisk.org/pages/Glossary.asp?SectionID=10). Microinsurance is the set of products and services that match the needs and capacity of microbusinesses and low-income households as a specific client target group.

Nonprudential regulation—This regulation is the set of government rules that apply to microfinance and that do not measure the financial soundness of the MFI. Examples include screening out unsuitable owners and managers or requiring transparent reporting and disclosure.

Outreach—Outreach is the scale of operations of a financial service provider, usually measured in terms of the number of active clients, active loan accounts, active savings accounts, or other measurements of client coverage.

Point-of-sale system—In terms of microfinance, the point-of-sale (POS) system consists of terminals that belong to a network shared by financial intermediaries. Clients from a number of institutions can use the same terminals and agents to make payments. Sharing network infrastructure enables financial institutions to achieve collectively the volume of transactions needed to cover the costs of the software, the hardware, and the connectivity required to provide distributed payments services. POS terminals generally use card swipe technology, bar code readers, and modems to transmit data from debit or credit cards to financial intermediaries, thus enabling financial transactions or the sale of products or services.

Prudential regulation—This regulation protects the financial soundness of an MFI to prevent it from losing depositors' money or damaging confidence in the financial system or both. Examples include capital-adequacy requirements and rules for provisioning for loan losses. MFIs subject to prudential regulations are sometimes referred to as "regulated MFIs," while MFIs subject only to nonprudential regulations are sometimes referred to as "nonregulated MFIs."

Risk management—Risk management is the structured approach to managing uncertainty related to a threat, by way of (1) identifying potential sources of loss, (2) measuring the financial consequences of a loss occurring, and (3) using controls to minimize actual loss or their financial consequences. Risk management strategies include transferring the risk to another party, avoiding the risk, reducing the negative effect of the risk, and accepting some or all of the consequences of a particular risk.

Supervision—the process of enforcement of government rules. Financial institutions that are licensed and monitored (supervised) by the government must comply with all requirements and regulations. If they comply, they can accept deposits from the public. Failure to comply may result in penalties or the loss of the banking license.

Triple bottom line—measurement of institutional success and sustainability according to three "bottom lines": economic, social, and environmental benefits.

Index

Boxes, figures, and tables are indicated by b, f, and t, respectively.

Eco-Audit

Environmental Benefits Statement

The World Bank is committed to preserving endangered forests and natural resources. The Office of the Publisher has chosen to print *Managing Risk and Creating Value with Microfinance* on 30 percent postconsumer recycled paper, processed chlorine free. The World Bank has formally agreed to follow the recommended standards for paper usage set by Green Press Initiative—a nonprofit program supporting publishers in using fiber that is not sourced from endangered forests. For more information, visit www.greenpressinitiative.org.

Managing Risk and Creating Value with Microfinance
146 pages x 1350 copies = 1700 lbs.
60# finch casa - 30% PCR

Total Savings Using 30% PCR Text Paper

Trees*	Solid Waste	Water	Net Greenhouse Gases	Power
7	183	3,021	627	2
*40' in height and 6-8" in diameter	Lbs.	Gallons	Lbs. CO_2 equiv.	million BTU's

green
press
INITIATIVE